Multi-party Democracy in the Maldives and the Emerging Security Environment in the Indian Ocean Region

Multi-party Democracy in the Maldives and the Emerging Security Environment in the Indian Ocean Region

ANAND KUMAR

INSTITUTE FOR DEFENCE STUDIES & ANALYSES
NEW DELHI

PENTAGON PRESS

Multi-party Democracy in the Maldives and the Emerging Security Environment in the Indian Ocean Region

Anand Kumar

First Published in 2016

ISBN 978-81-8274-895-8

Published by

PENTAGON PRESS
206, Peacock Lane, Shahpur Jat,
New Delhi-110049
Phones: 011-64706243, 26491568
Telefax: 011-26490600
email: rajan@pentagonpress.in
website: www.pentagonpress.in

In association with
Institute for Defence Studies and Analyses
No. 1, Development Enclave,
New Delhi-110010
Phone: +91-11-26717983
Website: www.idsa.in

Printed at Aegean Offset Printers, Greater Noida, U.P.

Contents

ACKNOWLEDGEMENTS

I am thankful to a large number of people who have been associated with this book from its inception. Space constraints may not allow me to acknowledge everyone individually. Some of them have also expressed a desire to remain anonymous because of the sensitive nature of their professions. However, a volume of this kind is not possible without the help of colleagues and friends. I would like to express my sincere thanks to Shri Jayant Prasad, Director General, Institute for Defence Studies and Analyses (IDSA), New Delhi, for his encouragement and support to bring out this volume. I am also thankful to Brig Rumel Dahiya, SM (Retd), Deputy Director General IDSA, for taking keen interest in the book. He played an important role in bringing out this book in a timely manner. The comments received from the anonymous referees were of great value and helped in improving the quality of the book. I am also grateful to Cdr. Aman Saberwal, a naval officer and colleague at IDSA, for going through two chapters of the book. I sincerely thank my colleagues at the South Asia Centre (IDSA) for their supportive role.

Among the people who requested anonymity are intelligence officials, members of the armed forces, senior government officers and human rights activists. I have also interviewed researchers, media persons, government officials, politicians and academicians in the Maldives who don't wish to be named. The inputs provided by them have been integrated in many places in the book.

I would also take this opportunity to thank Vivek Kaushik, Associate Editor at IDSA who put the book through its paces. Special thanks are also due to Ms. Nidhi Pant for copy-editing the manuscript in a professional and timely manner. Mr Rajan Arya, Mr Virender Negi and the staff of Pentagon Press also played an important role in publishing this volume on time.

My wife Nisha and children Yashi and Shaurya had to bear with my irregular schedules while the book was being written. This book is dedicated to them. I also take this opportunity to remember my uncle late Shri Kapil Deo Rai, who groomed me in my earlier years of life.

I hope this volume will contribute to a better understanding of the domestic politics and foreign policy of the Maldives and will also help to understand the great game that is being played in the Indian Ocean Region.

ANAND KUMAR

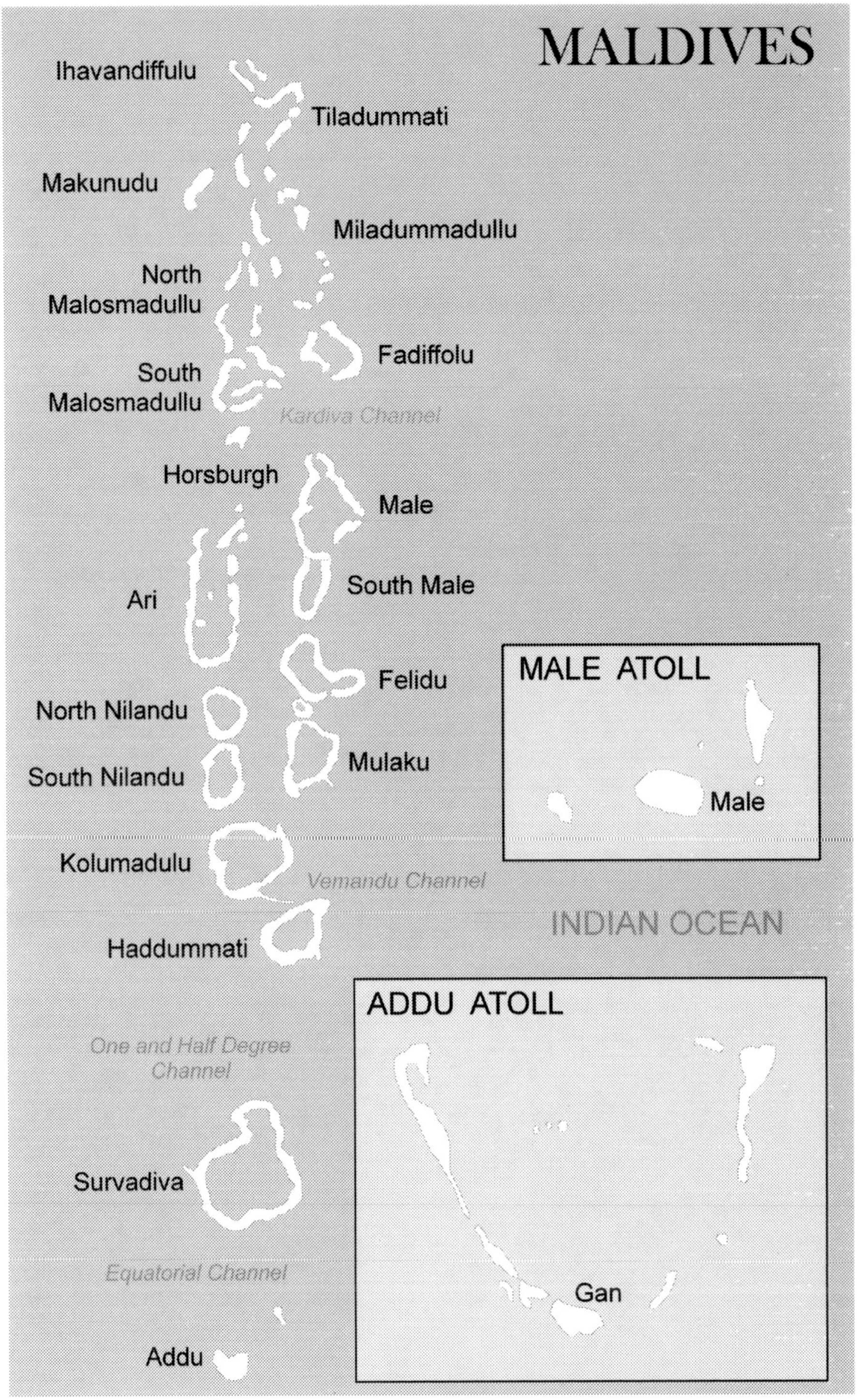
MALDIVES
Ihavandiffulu
Tiladummati
Makunudu
Miladummadullu
North Malosmadullu
Fadiffolu
South Malosmadullu
Kardiva Channel
Horsburgh
Male
Ari
South Male
Felidu
North Nilandu
South Nilandu
Mulaku
Kolumadulu
Vemandu Channel
Haddummati
One and Half Degree Channel
Survadiva
Equatorial Channel
Addu
MALE ATOLL
Male
INDIAN OCEAN
ADDU ATOLL
Gan

1

INTRODUCTION

The Maldivian islands are situated close to the south-western tip of the mainland India. The archipelago nation consists of 1192 islands out of which about 200 hundred are inhabited. The other remaining islands are used either for tourism or agriculture. Maldives is spread over roughly 90,000 square kilometres and is one of the world's most geographically dispersed countries. It is the smallest south Asian country in both land area and in population. The Maldivian islands have an average ground-level elevation of 1.5 meters above sea level that makes it the lowest country of the planet. Historically, this country has been linked to the Indian subcontinent. The constitution of the Maldives does not recognize any religion other than Islam and all Maldivians are supposed to be Sunni Muslims. Although under nominal Portuguese, Dutch, and British influences after the sixteenth century, Maldivians were left to govern themselves under a long line of Sultans and occasionally Sultanas. The capital city of the Maldives is known as Malé.

The islands gained independence from the United Kingdom in 1965, becoming a republic in 1968. Maldives became a member of the United Nation in 1965 and is one of the founding members of the South Asian Association for Regional Cooperation (SAARC). It is also a member of the Commonwealth of Nations, the Organization of Islamic Cooperation (OIC) and the Non-Aligned Movement. The country has presidential form of government. The Maldivian economy is dominated by tourism and fishing. The World Bank classifies the country as having an upper middle income economy.

The development of tourism started in the Maldives in 1970s, when the Maldivian government allowed the use of the uninhabited islands for this purpose. Tourism contributes in a big way in the Maldivian economy. However, these islands are kept separate and little interaction is allowed with people living in inhabited islands. This kind of arrangement helped the Maldives to practice conservative Islam and at the same time benefit from the tourism industry. This system worked well as long as the longest serving dictator of the Maldives, Maumoon Abdul Gayoom was in power. Gayoom had become president in 1978.

The winds of democracy however started blowing in the Maldives during the latter part of Gayoom's rule. The democratic movement in the Maldives challenged the then ruling Dhivehi Rayyithunge Party (Maldivian People's Party) of Gayoom and demanded democratic reform. The strongest challenge to Gayoom's rule came from the dissident journalist Mohamed Nasheed who was imprisoned 16 times for protesting against his regime. In 2003, Mohamed Nasheed founded the Maldivian Democratic Party (MDP) while in exile. His activism, as well as civil unrest that year, pressured Gayoom into allowing for gradual political reforms. A new constitution was written and approved. It also brought multi-party democracy in the Maldives in October 2008. Unfortunately, the first democratic government headed by former president Mohamed Nasheed could not complete its full term and was overthrown on February 7, 2012. Since then Maldives has been continuously in political turmoil.

The second multi-party election that was held in 2013 became controversial. It brought Abdulla Yameen, who is half-brother of former president Maumoon Abdul Gayoom to power. Many people believe that he does not truly represent popular will. Though the framework of democracy remains in the Maldives, significant changes seem to be taking place in its politics. The changes taking place in the Maldivian politics become important as they start affecting its foreign policy. It has been observed that all the three regimes that have come to power after the implementation of multi-party democracy followed different foreign policies which have implications for the security environment in the Indian Ocean region (IOR). The security environment of the IOR directly impinges on the Indian security.

The importance of the Maldives is because of its crucial geo-strategic location. It sits astride important Sea Lanes of Communication (SLOCs). The world's three major economies China, Japan and India depend for their energy supply on the Gulf oil. This further enhances the importance of the Maldives.

No doubt, the important geo-strategic location of the Maldives is an asset. But it also becomes problematic as it encourages a number of extra-regional players to meddle into its internal politics. The Indian Ocean has always been crucial to global connectivity and all world powers have sought their presence here. Now China too claims status of a global power. It also wants to be a maritime power. Now China's 'overseas interests', no longer means just protection of SLOCs.

To prevent Chinese from enhancing their influence in the Maldives, Americans are playing their own games. While they pay lip-service to the multi-party democracy in the Maldives, they tried to negotiate with President Mohamed Waheed Hassan Manik a Status of Forces Agreement (SOFA). According to the Maldivian pro-democracy movement, Waheed had come to power in a coup-d'état against Mohamed Nasheed. In short, in the great game for the control of the Indian Ocean the concern for democracy appeared to have been relegated to the background.

India has two main interests in the Maldives. It wants political stability in the country. It also wants to prevent the Maldives from falling under influences (both state and non-state) that are inimical to Indian security interests. The Indian foreign policy seems to be facing difficulty in meeting both these objectives.

The democratic transition in the Maldives was a very positive development, especially keeping in view the rising extremism in several Muslim countries. Unfortunately, this multi-party democracy soon started floundering, threatening not only the democracy of the Maldives but also the security environment of the whole Indian Ocean Region (IOR).

This book is an attempt to understand the fledgling multi-party democracy in the Maldives, its foreign policy and the evolving security scenario in the IOR.

Methodology

This research work has extensively used both primary as well as secondary sources. It uses material collected since 2005 on the Maldives. Media reports from the Maldives have been given precedence over international media reports, including Indian media. A field visit was also undertaken to the Maldives in 2011. This was the time when Mohamed Nasheed-led first democratic government was in power. During this field visit, top policy-makers, bureaucrats, officials of foreign ministry, journalists, researchers from non-governmental organisations and common people were interviewed. In some cases, the identities of people have not been disclosed as per their request. These interviews were quite useful in corroborating the media reports. The field visit also gave an opportunity to assess the situation prevailing in Maldives at firsthand.

Organisation

Apart from this introductory chapter (Chapter 1), this book comprises eight more chapters. Chapter 2 discusses the Maldives' road to multi-party democracy, in particular, an account of all the constitutions of the Maldives to date. Chapter 3 discusses Maldives' first tryst with multi-party democracy during Mohamed Nasheed's term as president, who came to power in 2008 after defeating Asia's longest-serving dictator, Maumoon Abdul Gayoom. The Maldives under the stop-gap regime of President Mohamed Waheed Hassan Manik is the subject of discussion in Chapter 4. Chapter 5 discusses the controversial second multi-party elections that raised questions about the survival of multi-party democracy in the Maldives. Chapter 6 deals with the Maldivian foreign policy under various regimes after the new Constitution was implemented in 2008. Chapter 7 discusses the strategic importance of the Indian Ocean and maritime challenges faced in this region, emphasising the strategic interests of active regional as well as extra-regional players – particularly China as the emerging maritime power. Chapter 8 attempts to understand the great game being played by powers-that-be in order to gain control of the Indian Ocean. The book concludes by dwelling upon the future of democracy in Maldives and its impact on the security environment in the IOR.

2

The Road to Multi-party Democracy

Multi-party democracy in Maldives is a new phenomenon. The country, however, already had several constitutions before this latest system of democracy became a reality. Interestingly, the process of constitutional development started in Maldives when the country was under British suzerainty, ruled by monarchs. It started voluntarily but was completed under public pressure when the sixth constitution actually brought multi-party democracy to the country.

Maldives and the British Suzerainty

The British took Sri Lanka under their control in 1789. Soon after, their influence also spread to the Maldives. This state of relationship between the British and the Maldivian Sultan, Musir-ud-din, was formalised in 1887 by a state agreement. According to this agreement, the Maldives came under British protection as a vassal state. This also meant an end to the long and almost unbroken period of independence of the Maldives.

Under the agreement of 1887, the Sultan recognised for himself and his successors the suzerainty of the British over the Maldives and disclaimed all rights or intentions to enter into a treaty with any foreign state, except Britain. The British on their part undertook to protect the Maldives against all foreign enemies while abstaining from interference in the local administration of the islands. However, despite this agreement of non-interference in local affairs, they, on occasion, did exercise discreet control, even applying a corrective influence in the affairs of the islands, particularly in matters of succession.

The First Written Constitution of the Maldives

The Maldives was under the rule of Sultan Mohamed Shamsudeen Iskandar III from 1903 to 1934. He is remembered as a remarkable ruler in the history of the Maldives as he himself decided to renounce his prerogatives and give the people a democratic constitution. He was perhaps inspired by the British who had given Sri Lanka a new constitution in 1931. On his initiative a 13-member committee began drafting the constitution on March 22, 1931. The then acting Governor of Ceylon, Bernard H. Bourdill, provided technical expertise in its composition. The first draft of the constitution was completed on June 16, 1931, and finally the first written constitution of the Maldives was codified on December 22, 1932.[1] With this the first semblance of representative government came into effect. The constitution required the King to be a sane man, from the Sunni Muslim faith, and belonging to the ruling family. It established a cabinet of ministers and a parliament comprising of 47 members.

The first constitution comprised 92 articles. It had a bill of rights guaranteeing equality before the law, freedom from arbitrary arrest and torture, protection of private property, freedom of expression, association and press, and pension after 25 years of service to the state.

No doubt, the first Maldivian constitution was a milestone, but it failed within nine months of ratification. It also made little difference to the people at large. All the high offices of government were held by persons who belonged to the aristocracy. In its short tenure the newly established unicameral legislature called the People's Majlis passed 40 laws. The new legislation established fines, penalised theft and assault, created a state trading company and regulated foreign trade through the Foreign Investments Act and Freighters Act. The common public and influential foreign traders who controlled the import of food were angered by the new legislation and started a series of strikes on July 26, 1933. They demanded repeal of the new government's policies.

The ensuing food insecurity led to a public revolt. The Sultan himself was accused of wilful interference in the administration of justice. This led to his dethronement in 1934, in accordance with his own constitution. The founders of the constitution were banished to Colombo. In June 1934, the constitution was amended to 84 articles. Subsequently, in 1937 it was reduced to 80 articles before being finally suspended in 1940 after the World War II broke out. A special Majlis at that time stated that "the Constitution and General Provisions were annulled as they [did] not fit the Maldives' situation."

The Second Constitution

Hassan Nooradeen, son of Sultan Musir-ud-din, who had concluded the 1887 Agreement with the British, was formally placed on the throne in 1938. On April 23, 1942, Sultan Hassan Nooradeen sent a 17-article constitution to the Majlis, saying he wanted "a suitable constitution to exist in the Maldives". The "small constitution" handed the powers of the state to the monarchy, the foreign minister, and the People's Majlis. The People's Majlis was reduced to six appointed members and 27 elected members. The second constitution was amended in 1951; it reinstated freedom from arbitrary arrest and banishment and freedom of expression, speech, and association. The term of the 34-member People's Majlis was set to five years.

Establishment of First Republican Government with the Third Constitution

In 1945, Sultan Abdul Majid Didi was elected in accordance with the constitution, but his ill-health did not permit him to perform his duties and his powers were vested in a Regency Council headed by Al-Ameer Mohamed Ameen Dhoshimeyna Kilegefaanu (popularly known as Mohamed Ameen Didi). In 1948 Ceylon became independent and Maldives became a protectorate of the British. The British government signed a new agreement with the Maldives. This agreement stated that the Maldives would remain under the protection of the British crown and its external affairs were to be conducted by or in accordance with the advice of the British government. Britain however was to refrain from interfering in the internal affairs of the islands. The Maldivian Sultan was to afford such facilities for British forces as were necessary for the defence of the islands or the Commonwealth. No tribute was to be paid by Maldives. Interestingly, the British did not find it necessary to register the 1948 agreement under article 102 of UN Charter on grounds that only agreements between international persons needed to be registered while the Sultan of the Maldivian Islands was "not an international personality at all."[2]

Sultan Abdul Majid Didi died on 21 February 1952. Subsequently, the People's Majlis voted to abolish the monarchy and institute a republican government in the Maldives. A public referendum endorsed the change. This ended 836 years of Sultanate rule. On January 1, 1953, a third constitution established a presidential system of government in the Maldives for the first time. The new democratic constitution, comprising 30 articles, provided provisions for a president elected by direct vote, a judiciary appointed by the president and a bicameral legislature – an 18-member senate and a 47-member House of Representatives. Moreover, the new constitution limited the presidential term to five years, and appointed Al-Ameer Mohamed Ameen Dhoshimeyna Kilegefaanu (Mohamed Ameen Didi) as the first president of the Maldives. He served as the head of government between January 1, 1953 and August 21, 1953.

On January 1, 1953 Britain signed a treaty with the Maldives giving recognition to a new republic. On behalf of the British, Sir Cecil Syers, the British High Commissioner in Sri Lanka signed this treaty. It is important to note that despite the Maldives becoming a republic, Britain remained the suzerain power and the Maldives was not yet independent.[3] Thus, it did not mean much to the people who continued to have limited rights.

Alongside the declaration of the Maldives as a Republic, the pact with Britain on defence and foreign affairs was also renewed in 1953 with an added clause which gave Britain the explicit right "after consultation with the Government of the Maldive Islands," to set up military facilities on Maldivian territory. With decolonisation taking place in South Asia Britain was apprehensive about losing its military effectiveness in this region. The worst fears of Britain came true in 1956 when Sri Lanka expressed its inability to allow the continuation of British military presence on its Trincomalee harbour and Katunayake airport. Britain tried to use the Maldives as a substitute but with little success.

The regime of Mohamed Ameen Didi however soon became unpopular for a number of reasons. His certain measures of taxation were not liked by the people of the Maldives. There was also extreme shortage of food (partly due to heavy Monsoon) leading to virtual famine in which suspicion was rife that the President was making capital along with the Borah merchants.[4] This regime is also known for the progressive steps that the Sultan undertook for the liberation of women in the Maldives. He removed the "purdah" system and unveiled women participated in the ceremonies of government formation. The high walls created in Maldivian houses to shield women were pulled down on his order.[5] For the first time in Maldivian history, a woman was elected to the parliament.

The steps taken by the first president, Ameen Didi, for the emancipation of women and his other reforms were resented by more conservative elements among the people, and few months later he was overthrown on August 21, 1953. His cousins Muhammad Farid Didi and Ibrahim Ali Didi became co-presidents in September 1953. The people's Majlis voted for return to the old system, and the Maldives reverted to a Sultanate on January 31, 1954.

The Fourth Constitution Brings Elected Monarchy

The change in the Maldivian political system, that is, a return to the Sultanate, was followed by the ratification of the fourth Constitution on March 7, 1954. The fourth constitution declared the Maldives to be an "elected monarchy". A unicameral legislature was reinstated with 54 members, of which six were to represent the King, 46 the people and two the businessmen. Only Maldivian men could vote to elect the People's Majlis. On 7 March 1954, Muhammad Farid Didi, was installed as new Sultan at Malé, and Ibrahim Ali Didi became the prime minister in new government.

Muhammad Farid Didi and Ibrahim Ali Didi were amicable to British interests in the region. British who were looking for an alternative to Sri Lanka so that they can conveniently connect to Australia and the Far East signed an agreement with the Maldives in 1956. This agreement allowed use of Gan Island as an airfield and Hittadu as a radio-communication centre for a period of 100 years, as a "free gift." This agreement was however not ratified by the Maldivian parliament where it came under heavy attack by the opposition members in 1958. The opposition demanded construction to be suspended until an agreement had been finalised.

Meanwhile, Prime Minister Ibrahim Ali Didi had resigned for the health reasons and in his place Ibrahim Nasir came to power who was a very dynamic person. Nasir refused to sign the agreement already initiated between the British government and the former Prime Minister. It was felt that the terms of agreement violated the sovereignty and independence of the Maldives and was in nature of an "occupation of Addu Attol by British forces without the consent of the people of Maldives." Nasir managed to renegotiate the agreement in favour of Maldives. British rights over the Addu atoll were further reduced to 30 years from 100 years by the 1960 agreement. Malé also received a payment of $100,000 and was promised another $75000 over a period of five years for development works.

The Gan problem however was far from solved and it continued to invigorate Maldivian demand for sovereign independence. By the end of 1963, pressure was increased for complete independence of the Maldives as a condition for continuing the facilities enjoyed by Britain in the island state. Maldives won its independence from the British Empire on 26 July 1965 and shortly after it the fourth constitution was repealed.

Establishment of Second Republic with the Fifth Constitution

A Second Republic was established under the rule of President Ibrahim Nasir in 1968, who had increasingly dominated the political scene. The new constitution declared the Maldives to be "an independent and free state". The country was now renamed, "the Republic of Maldives". According to the fifth constitution, the President of the Maldives was to be elected through a secret vote of the 54-member People's Majlis.

The President had full executive authority and was to be assisted by a council of ministers appointed by him. Ministers were not necessarily to be chosen from among the members of the Majlis. In addition to the council of ministers, or "Ministers' Majlis", as it was called, there was also a Citizens' Majlis of 48 members, 38 of whom were elected, two from each of the 19 atolls and two from Malé. Eight members were appointed by the President.

In February 1972, the constitution was further amended and a new post of Prime Minister was created. The executive powers were transferred from the President to the Prime Minister. Ahmed Zaki, who was then Minister for External Affairs, was voted to the office of the Prime Minister and assumed charge in August 1972. In 1973, Ibrahim Nasir was re-elected President for a second term of office for a period of five years; Ahmed Zaki continued as the Prime Minister.

Special Majlis was convened to meet in April 1975 to consider amendments to the 1968 Constitution. The Special Majlis decided inter alia to abolish the office of the Prime Minister and to create offices of four vice-presidents with executive powers. Further changes were introduced by the Majlis in 1977 when the four vice-presidents were re-designated Ministers and a new Ministry of Tourism and Foreign Investment was also added.[6] In 1978, President Nasir indicated his intention of not seeking re-election for a third term. The Special Majlis was then convened, and it elected Maumoon Abdul Gayoom, the then Transport Minister, to the office of President. The new President took office in November 1978. Gayoom virtually served as a dictator for the next thirty years.

During this period the elections to the Majlis were held once in every five years and there was universal suffrage. There were no political parties in the Maldives and members of the Majlis were often elected on the basis of programmes of action put forward by them individually. The judiciary was independent of the Majlis and the Chief Justice was appointed by the President. Justice under the Sharia or Islamic law was administered in the atolls by Kazis who were also appointed by the President. Whipping or exile to distant islands was the punishment most often used.

In 1980, the second President of the Second Republic, Maumoon

Abdul Gayoom, called for a special constitutional assembly consisting of cabinet ministers and People's Majlis members to amend the new constitution. After an 18-year-long process, the fifth constitution of the Maldives was amended for the fourth time. Notable amendments included clauses permitting any individual who wished to stand for presidency to submit an application to the People's Majlis. The Majlis would then choose a candidate who then had to be approved through a public referendum.

Establishment of Constitutional Assembly by Gayoom

In September 2003, unprecedented anti-government riots broke out in Malé, sparked by deaths of four prison inmates. These riots happened shortly after the Majlis had unanimously endorsed President Gayoom as the sole candidate for a record sixth term in office. In October 2003, Gayoom was elected by 90.3 per cent of the popular vote. In his inaugural address, Gayoom promised various political reforms. Gayoom's first steps were to institute a human rights commission in 2003 to investigate abuses and establish a constitutional assembly in May 2004 to draft a democratic constitution. The constitution was to guarantee separation of powers and multi-party democracy in the Maldives.

The constitutional assembly – the People's Special Majlis – consisted of 29 appointees, along with 42 elected members of the regular Majlis and a further 29 elected members. The drafting process was slow as the rival parties were at loggerheads with each other over several issues. The opposition had proposed adoption of a parliamentary system in the Maldives. However, the issue was decided by a public referendum in August 2007 where the 60 per cent of the public voted for a presidential system of government.

The 2008 Constitution

The sixth constitution of the Maldives was ratified in August 2008. It introduced a whole new set of democratic rights, separation of powers and mechanisms for accountability and transparency. The powers of the judiciary were statutorily demarcated from those of the head of state.[7] It paved the way for Maldives' first multi-party elections in October 2008.

The 2008 Constitution provides for an executive president and a legislature, the People's Majlis, both elected directly every five years by universal suffrage. The president can serve a maximum of two terms in office. The Majlis comprises two elected members from each of the 20 administrative atolls and Malé. Where the residents registered in an administrative atoll exceed 5,000, one additional member is provided for each group of 5,000 in excess of the first 5,000. In April 2014, the Majlis had 85 members. All elections are run on a multi-party platform. The Constitution provides for an independent judiciary where judicial power is vested in the courts with the Supreme Court as the court of last resort.

Basic rights and freedoms, including freedom of the media, of assembly and of association, are guaranteed as fundamental rights: freedom of expression is guaranteed so long as it does not violate any tenet of Islam.[8]

The Constitution provides for separate independent commissions whose objective is to defend judicial independence, conduct elections, prevent and combat corruption, promote human rights and ensure an effective and efficient civil service.

NOTES

1. "A Short Constitutional History of the Maldives," *Minivan News*, December 22, 2013, at http://minivannews.com/comment-2/a-short-constitutional-history-of-the-maldives-73902.
2. Urmila Phadnis, Ela Dutt Luithui,"Maldives: Winds of Change in an Atoll State," South Asian Publishers Pvt. Ltd. 1985, p. 25
3. V. H. Coelho, "Constitutional and Political Development in the Maldives," *Foreign Affairs Reports*, XXVIII (8), August 1979, p. 141.
4. Urmila Phadnis, Ela Dutt Luithui,"Maldives: Winds of Change in an Atoll State," p. 26
5. "Great Britain Signs Treaty Recognizing New Republic," *The Evening Citizen*, Ottawa, Canada, January 2, 1953.
6. Ibid., p. 144.
7. "Transition to Multi-party Democracy," *Economic and Political Weekly*, 43 (47), November 22-28, 2008, p. 7.
8. "Maldives: Constitution and Politics," The Commonwealth, at http://thecommonwealth.org/our-member-countries/maldives/constitution-politics.

3

Multi-party Democracy in the Maldives

Multi-party democracy was ushered in the Maldives with the passage of the latest constitution on August 7, 2008. This enabled the country to hold democratic elections before the term of erstwhile dictator, and President, Maumoon Abdul Gayoom, ended. This development was possible for two reasons. First, the process was expedited because of the spirited fight of the unofficial MDP members and a no-nonsense Speaker of the Special Majlis, Gasim Ibrahim. Second, in some measure it was also because the former President, Gayoom, despite having all the powers, did not try to block a completely new constitution. However, at the same time, he ensured that the constitution did not bar him from contesting again.

Presidential Election 2008

Tables 1 and 2 provide the official result for the first and second rounds of 2008 presidential elections, respectively.

Onset of Multi-party Democracy

The presidential elections held on the basis of the new 2008 Constitution brought to power Mohamed Nasheed, and caused the exit of Maumoon

Table 1: Official Result for the First Round of Presidential Elections Held on October 8, 2008

#	*Full Name*	*Permanent Address*	*Votes Received*	*Percentage*
1	Gasim Ibrahim	M. Maafannu Villa, Malé	27,056	15.32
2	Uz. Maumoon Abdul Gayyoom	MA. Kinmbigasdhoshuge, Malé	71,731	40.63
3	Dr Hassan Saeed	Dhiggaagasdhoshuge, S. Feydhoo	29,633	16.78
4	Mohamed Nasheed	G. Kenereege, Malé	44,293	25.09
5	Ibrahim Ismail	MA. Boagan Villa, Malé	1,382	0.78
6	Umar Naseer	H. Dhonjaymuge, Malé	2,472	1.40
	Total valid votes		176,567	
	Total invalid votes		1,235	
	Total number of eligible voters		208,252	

Source: Elections Commission, Republic of Maldives, at http://www.elections.gov.mv/presidentialelectionsresults2008.html.

Table 2: Official Result for the Second Round of Presidential Elections Held on October 28, 2008

#	*Full Name*	*Permanent Address*	*Votes Received*	*Percentage*
1	Uz. Maumoon Abdul Gayyoom	MA. Kinmbigasdhoshuge, Malé	82,121	45.79
2	Mohamed Nasheed	G. Kenereege, Malé	97,222	54.21
	Total valid votes		179, 343	
	Total invalid votes		1,861	
	Total number of eligible voters		209,294	

Source: Elections Commission, Republic of Maldives, at http://www.elections.gov.mv/presidentialelectionsresults2008.html.

Abdul Gayoom. The transition to multi-party democracy after the elections was smooth. The country also got an opportunity to consolidate this democracy a year later in 2009 when the parliamentary elections were held. Unfortunately, the outcome of the parliamentary elections instead of consolidating democracy only made it fragile, as the later events were to show.

The 2009 Parliamentary Elections

The first multi-party elections for the Maldivian Parliament (the Majlis) were held on May 9, 2009.[1] In these elections 458 candidates took part. The Maldivian Democratic Party (MDP) put up 76 candidates, 56 were from Gayoom's Dhivehi Rayyithunge Party (DRP), 17 from the Republican Party, four from the Adhaalath Party, and five from the Islamic Democratic Party (IDP). Gayoom's half-brother and leader of the People's Alliance (PA), Abdulla Yameen, also put up some candidates. Besides, a large number of independent candidates were in the fray.

The MDP failed to get a majority in these elections. The DRP combined with the PA emerged as a very strong opposition with just four seats short of a simple majority.[2] Still, the election results were not seen as a setback for Nasheed, the leader of the MDP. This kind of verdict was expected as the MDP did not fight these elections in a coalition. The presence of numerous candidates in the fray had ensured that the MDP would not sweep the polls. In the Maldivian system power is divided between the president and the parliament and the lack of majority for Nasheed in the parliament created hurdles for him in governance as the opposition was not so well-disposed towards him.

Parties like the Adhaalath Party and Islamic Democratic Party (IDP) who placed too much emphasis on religion lost. Several smaller parties were washed out. The MDP vote share increased incrementally, but Maldives remained far from becoming a two-party system (see Table 3).

Nasheed probably underestimated the influence of Gayoom who along with his half-brother emerged as a formidable opposition. Nasheed also made the mistake of thinking that the bitterness between him and the opposition had disappeared permanently after he won the presidential election in 2008.

This understanding of Nasheed about the opposition parties, in particular Gayoom's party, that they would cooperate with the new government was probably based on the bonhomie that existed at that time between him and the former President. In a press conference held on the eve of Nasheed taking over as president, Gayoom actually exhorted people to embrace the changes in the spirit of unity and nationalism, forgetting past rivalry and differences. Things however started changing once Nasheed was in power; both Nasheed and Gayoom moved on to different trajectories giving rise to a long-lasting political rivalry.

Table 3: Results of the May 9, 2009 Maldivian Parliamentary Elections at a Glance

Party	*Votes*	*Vote Share (%)*	*Number of Seats*
Dhivehi Rayyithunge Party	40,886	24.62	28
Maldivian Democratic Party	51,184	30.81	26
People's Alliance	8,283	4.99	7
Dhivehi Qaumee Party	5,854	3.52	2
Republican Party	7,001	4.22	1
Justice Party	1,487	0.90	-
Social Liberal Party	674	0.41	-
Gaumee Itthihaad	518	0.31	-
Islamic Democratic Party	214	0.13	-
Maldives National Congress	119	0.07	-
DFP	50	0.03	-
Independents	49,835	30.00	13
Total	166,105	100.00	77

Source: Election Commission of the Maldives, as quoted in http://en.wikipedia.org/wiki/Maldivian_parliamentary_election,_2009.

Emergence of the Political Rivalry

Despite failing to get a majority in the parliament, Nasheed gave the impression that it was a good thing to happen which would help to keep the government accountable. Unfortunately, soon Nasheed faced a practical problem when the opposition started frustrating his every move and created hurdles in running the country.

The members of the new Majlis took oath on May 19, 2009. Former foreign minister Abdulla Shaeed of DRP was elected as the Speaker while the post of Deputy Speaker went to Ahmed Nazim of PA. Both of them had a tainted past and were adversely commentated upon in the Auditor General's report for financial irregularities.

In the changed political situation, Gayoom went back on his earlier promise of cooperation with the government. Moreover, though Gayoom had received all the privileges and monetary support from the government, he was looking for immunity for his past acts of alleged corruption and misuse of authority, which the government was not willing to grant. As a result, Nasheed faced difficulty in implementing his policies and programmes. The opposition did not allow the government to pass even a single bill in the first three-month-long session of the Majlis that ended in September 2009.

Things somewhat improved for the government when four Members of Parliament (MPs) from other parties including the foreign Minister, Dr. Ahmed Shaheed, decided to support the ruling party. This however couldn't last long and soon after the Dhivehi Qauvmee Party (DQP) led by former Attorney General, Dr. Hassan Saeed, withdrew its support to the government. DQP was founded in January 2009 by Dr. Hassan Saeed along with the then foreign Minister, Dr. Ahmed Shaheed, and Dr. Mohammed Jameel. They had also wholeheartedly supported President Nasheed in the run-off to the second round of the 2008 Presidential elections.

The simmering differences came out in the open when Dr. Hassan Saeed openly called for the resignation of the Finance Minister for his poor performance. Subsequently, DQP also withdrew support to Nasheed and alleged MDP for irresponsible behaviour and not consulting its allies. The exit of DQP from the government forced the Foreign Minister, Ahmed Shaheed, to leave the DQP and join the MDP in October 2009. He justified this step by saying that it was time to strengthen the government which he considered as the vanguard of democracy in the Maldives. He pointed out that his association with the MDP would help advance its agenda.[3]

At least during the initial days of his term, Nasheed gave political freedom to the opposition and refrained from being vindictive. When the opposition threatened to carry out island-wide demonstrations in the first week of November 2008, Nasheed stated in a party meeting that he would not stop them from holding demonstrations against the government. He was unwilling to resort to the same oppressive measures that he and his party had faced during the former regime of Gayoom.

Nasheed Gives up 'Forgive and Forget' Policy

Once the 2009 parliamentary elections were over, the then President, Nasheed, took some hard decisions which became controversial. He sacked one of his cabinet ministers, two senior and experienced army officers, and his Attorney General. While he was perfectly justified in sacking the Attorney General Fathimath Dhiyana Saeed in May 2009 for her out-of-turn remarks that were made public even before these reached the President, the sacking of the Minister for Civil Aviation and Communications, Dr. Mohamed Jameel, and the army officers appeared to be for reasons other than their inefficiency. Jameel had earlier alleged in the media about the government's disregard for the constitution and the appointment of atoll and island councillors, who were allegedly influencing the electorate. Another controversy was created when he formed a six-member investigative commission on May 17, 2009 to investigate into embezzlement of state funds, fraud, and corruption.

The opposition party, DRP, called it foul play and termed the order as unconstitutional, saying that the president was not authorised to establish commissions which could issue arrest warrants. The party alleged that it was a veiled attempt to harass and defame senior PA and DRP leaders like ex-President Gayoom. They also termed it as an "erosion of democracy". The allegation of the opposition was however unjustified as the Maldivian Constitution does allow the president to appoint temporary commissions to advise him on national issues and to conduct investigations.

Ironically, the DRP tried to project itself as a champion of democracy after its 30 years of dictatorial rule, and Gayoom accused the Nasheed government of regressing from the democratic ideals established under his rule. He called upon the Parliament to hold the government accountable, and also lodged a complaint with the Human Rights Commission of Maldives about the treatment being meted out to him.

President Nasheed's new strategy of constituting the investigative commission indicated a departure from his "forget and forgive" policy, which he had adopted immediately after winning the elections. The strategy was certainly risky for him as Gayoom despite his despotic rule enjoyed significant support in the Maldives, and had allowed a smooth transition.

Moreover, it could have easily disturbed the smooth functioning of the government, which to a large extent it finally did.

There were two possible reasons for the change in policy. First, the enormity of the embezzlement of the state funds was such that it was difficult for President Nasheed to ignore it. Second, Nasheed's colleagues were also putting pressure on him to prosecute Gayoom, who after having obtained all the privileges as a "former president" was repeatedly criticising the government on all issues. Many of them had also suffered under his regime.

While there were many cases of diversion and misuse of funds over a period of time, the 2007 audit report of the government particularly revealed waste, fraud, and money laundering. The report of the Auditor General, Ibrahim Naeem (served from January 16, 2008 to March 29, 2010), showed widespread fraudulent practices by government officials who cooked books and fudged documents. There were serious instances of corruption on the supply side, too.

Further, the 2008 budget had an unacceptable deficit of Rf 4 billion, and according to the Auditor General, it was not a balanced one. He also informed that his warnings were not heeded and the dollar shortage existing in the country was directly related to the imbalanced budget. Thus, the former government was directly seen responsible for the severe economic crisis of Maldives in 2009.

Finally, the Presidential commission formally summoned Gayoom to its office on July 12, 2009 to probe into alleged embezzlement and corruption of state funds and resources. The investigation into the massive corruption scandal certainly lowered the status of the former president; however, in addition, it also created an environment of confrontation between the ruling MDP and the opposition.

Power Struggle between the President and the Parliament

Multi-party democracy was established in the Maldives with the implementation of the new constitution in 2008.[4] However, the institutions that were supposed to give strength to democracy remained weak. Undoubtedly, it was clear even before the new system came into being that a mere change in government would not necessarily bring in democracy. What was required was to build working institutions, modernise the political system, strengthen oversight mechanism, and overhaul the criminal justice system, including the writing of a new penal code.[5]

However, the Maldives instead saw disruptive partisan politics from May 2009. The MDP could not get a majority in the parliament. As a result, the control of the parliament shifted to the opposition parties, DRP and PA, which altogether had 35 seats in the 77-member house. Ultimately, a series of bitter disputes started between the executive and legislative branches.

The week position of the government prompted the opposition parties to start street protests leading to political unrest in the country. A private radio channel, DhiFM, aired live interviews with the opposition leaders where they called on people to participate in protests and overthrow the government.[6]

Moreover, the Criminal Court of the Maldives acquitted Adam Naseer, one of the six alleged drug dealers in the country, in February 2010 leading to widespread public outrage. The government admitted that it was unable to act against such drug dealers despite knowing their identity because they were closely linked to the opposition parties and any action against them would be interpreted as politically motivated.

Another clash emerged between the opposition-dominated Public Accounts Committee (PAC) and the Auditor General, Ibrahim Naeem, over charges of corruption in 2010. Though Ibrahim Naeem was appointed by former President Gayoom and approved by a parliament controlled by the DRP, he gave a number of damning audit reports alleging rampant corruption under the former administration. The DRP refuted these allegations on grounds of bias and questioned the strategic release of audit reports, as key reports were made public days before the parliamentary elections. The PAC on the other hand wanted Naeem dismissed on corruption charges for using the official credit card for personal purposes and not reimbursing the payment. Naeem claimed that these charges were made with the objective to discredit his office and prevent him from reclaiming the stolen money stored in overseas bank accounts. He was however dismissed by the parliament (on March 29, 2010) a day after the meeting of the Maldives Partnership Forum where donors had pledged a total sum of US$ 487 million.[7]

The opposition also managed to scuttle the MDP's attempt to group the existing 21 administrative atolls into seven provinces with the objective of achieving economy of scale.[8] The opposition argued that provincial councils in place of atoll councils would lead to disproportionate representation marginalising less populous, smaller atolls. It got a legislation passed to this effect which devolved decisionmaking powers to elected island and atoll councils.

Further, another tussle ensued between the president and the parliament over the appointment of the new Supreme Court bench. The opposition-dominated Judicial Service Commission (JSC) reappointed almost all sitting judges despite vocal opposition from President Nasheed's appointee to the JSC, Aishath Velezinee, and concerns about the competence and integrity of a number of judges appointed under the former government, when former president Gayoom was the head of the judiciary.[9]

Other Challenges before Nasheed's Government

Two major challenges beset Nasheed's government. First, he had taken over at a time of global recession. Moreover, the financial crisis in the Maldives was made worse because of the earlier profligate and corruption-ridden Gayoom regime. Second, this was also the time when many Muslim countries, including the Maldives, were facing the problem of Islamic fundamentalism.

A Legacy of Financial Crisis

In 2008, Nasheed had inherited an almost bankrupt government. He made this very clear when a World Bank delegation visited him. The country did not even have the minimum fiscal reserve required under the Constitution. The national debt was $ 471.7 million in 2008, and was expected to go up. This was approximately 45 per cent of the Gross Domestic Product (GDP). The fiscal deficit rose to 13¾ per cent of the GDP in 2008, reflecting rapid increases in current expenditures, particularly in the wage bill, combined with a fall in tourism-related revenue in the second half of 2008, driven by the global downturn. In 2009, additional increases in salaries and wages drove up spending, while revenues reduced further as the global crisis unfolded.

The magnitude of the financial crisis in the country was so great that President Nasheed decided not to attend the "Copenhagen Summit" in December 2009 as a follow up to the Kyoto Protocol, notwithstanding his commitment to fighting climate change. Subsequently, however, the United Nations (UN) came forward to finance his trip to Copenhagen (and earlier to New York in February 2009, too, for a UN meeting).

Though global recession was partly responsible for the Maldives' economic woes, there were also a number of factors which were peculiar to the country. The salaries of government employees were increased. The previous government had also started construction work without making adequate provisions. These liabilities had to be borne by the new government. The previous government had appointed a large number of incapable people in senior positions with fat salaries, and was managing it by resorting to deficit budgeting. Besides, the country had to spend money on three elections in quick succession. Subsequently, investigation by the Presidential Commission revealed more details about Gayoom's profligate habits, including huge expenses including stay at expensive hotels, medical treatment for family members, and loans to the President's office personnel and relatives.

The International Monetary Fund (IMF) also sent a delegation in June 2009 to take stock of the economic situation in the Maldives. This delegation felt that Nasheed's government could have done little to insulate the country from the global economic crisis. It estimated that the global economic slowdown would make country's GDP come down by 4.5 per cent. The Maldivian economy revolves around fish exports and tourism. Both these sectors were showing a downtrend.

The grave economic situation forced President Nasheed to take some desperate measures which also made the government somewhat unpopular. Steps were taken to control government expenditure. Cabinet ministers were directed to reduce the wages in their departments by 20 per cent. Various departments were told not to hire private buildings for the government or for the departments under them. The government contemplated moving some of its offices away from Malé to reduce expenditure. It also contemplated reduction in the number of political appointees and civil servants. It closed down several mosques specially built for women to reduce the expenditure, with the Deputy Minister for Islamic affairs arguing that in Islam the best place for women to pray was at home.

The government however could not succeed in reducing the salaries of the MPs who were getting Rf 62,500 (US$ 4800) per month. Cutting across party lines, the members joined hands and defeated the proposal. Some of the ruling party members also voted against the reduction.

The government had some reduction plans for the bureaucracy as well. In 2008/9, the number of civil servants in the Maldives was about 32,000, about 12 per cent of the total population. Nasheed felt that this ratio was very high. He wanted to reduce this number by half. The government estimated that roughly 12,000 government employees were redundant. However, this line of thinking was bound to create resentment in the country.

Nevertheless, the financial crisis forced the government to reduce the salaries and allowances of civil servants by 15 per cent in October 2009. The opposition objected to this salary cut, and Nasheed's suggestion that the cuts would be restored with the improvement in economy was not accepted. The opposition used various independent commissions including the Civil Service Commission (CSC) to undermine the authority of the government. This led to several clashes between government bodies and institutions which made functioning of the government quite difficult. A group of MPs belonging to DRP, PA, and IDP filed a petition before the CSC to reject the government's efforts to lay off civil servants or to reduce their pay and allowances. Even the Human Rights Commission of the Maldives sided with the bureaucracy and urged the government not to reduce the allowances – a testament to the bureaucracy's clout.

The CSC took the Ministry of Finance and Treasury to court over the government's refusal to restore slashed salaries for civil servants. The CSC argued that the government had agreed to review the cuts every three months and restore the earlier salary once annual government revenue exceeded Rf 7 billion (US$ 545 million). The Finance Ministry accused the independent commission of pursuing "a hidden political agenda" to cause economic distress and topple the government. The civil court's eventual verdict in favour of the CSC was appealed by the government at the High Court.[10]

To improve the economic condition, the government planned some economic measures. It contemplated various long-term lease of islands for development and fisheries. Nasheed also approached international financial institutions for help. The IMF approved a total of $ 92.5 million in financing to help the country tackle economic problems arising from the global downturn. The World Bank and the European Union (EU) Investment Bank also agreed to provide financial assistance.

The Government of India had initially offered a loan of $ 100 million. But this amount was substantially raised when a delegation from the Export-Import Bank of India visited Maldives on July 1, 2009. It offered a substantial $ 300-million loan to the Maldivian private sector with government backing. Of this, $ 50 million was to be spent in health and education sectors. Half the loan was to be spent on public-private partnership programmes in sewage management, road, and harbour facilities.

Notwithstanding Nasheed's efforts to bail the Maldives out of a severe crisis that was not of his own making, his attempts to bring the fiscal deficit down did not succeed. Moreover, economic difficulties provided no time for Nasheed to make progress on some of his pet schemes like restructuring the country, a national health scheme with a graduated health insurance for all, reduction in drug trafficking and drug addiction, social protection for the disadvantaged people, and providing housing to the people, particularly in Malé.

Economic Crisis Alienated People

Though economic crisis was a legacy of the Gayoom era, its impact was felt when Nasheed was in power. Unfortunately, Nasheed and his team failed to improve the situation after taking over. The Maldives' economy runs on tourism and fisheries. Both these sectors were not doing well. The tourism industry was facing a problem because of the economic downturn in the West. Even though during this period the Chinese tourists did fill the void, it was a poor substitute for the reduced number of Western tourists. The resort owners were barely able to make any profit.[11]

The Dollar crisis deepened in Maldives as economy worsened. Maldives is largely an import-based economy. The shortage of dollar led to the devaluation of the Maldivian currency. For a large number of Maldivians who go abroad for medical treatment and education, it meant higher costs – they now had to spend more Rufiya to buy the same amount of dollars.[12] The soaring prices of essential goods, too, created difficulties for the Maldivian people and led to Nasheed's declining popularity.

Rise of Islamic Fundamentalism

Islamic extremism was yet another challenge that the Nasheed government had to face. In the past, the Maldives had been a moderate Islamic country, but in recent years, the country has seen an increase in Islamic radicalism. This is partly because of the current global trend and partly because of the local dynamics. Though the ground for radicalism was laid during the regime of Gayoom, he managed to keep a check on the phenomenon. Ironically, a spurt in radicalism was witnessed when the first democratic government under Mohamed Nasheed took over power. Actually, Islamists played an important role in the overthrow of his government.

Emergence of Religious Extremism in the Maldives

The Maldives is a 100 per cent Sunni Muslim country that follows the Shafi School.[13] The Maldivian Islam however contains a number of local cultural practices. Traditionally, women in Maldives did not cover their faces or heads. Men did not grow beards. Interaction between men and women was allowed. Arranged marriage, which is the norm in most Muslim societies, was not practised here. This situation seemed to have changed in the last few decades (especially after 2005) and a more puritan Islam started growing in influence in the country. One can now easily find burqa-clad women and bearded men on the streets of Malé.

Two contradictory set of ideas took root in the Maldives in the 1970s. This was the period when tourism was expanded as industry and Western tourists with secular outlook started coming to the islands. Many

Maldivians also went to Western universities to study and returned with progressive ideas.

At the same time, conservative ideologies also arrived in the islands. They were ultra-conservative religious ideas of Saudi Wahabism and South Asian Deobandism. They also entered through the route of education and travel. Saudi Arabia financially supported the development of Wahabi religious study in the islands, and the College of Islamic Studies was founded in Malé in 1980.[14] In April 2014, Pakistan's Roznama Ummat reported that Saudis are "thinking of building a base consisting of three islands" as well as mosques and madrassas with Pakistani manpower.[15]

Due to shortage of good educational opportunities in the Maldives, many parents send their children to study theology in madrassas of Saudi Arabia and Pakistan. Most of these madrassas are unregulated and propagate radical and extremist teachings. On their return, these youngsters often become paragons of religious extremism.[16]

Gayoom and the Islamic Extremists

The roots of emerging Islamic extremism in the Maldives are often traced to the Gayoom era and to his policies of "Islamification". Though Gayoom was not an extremist, he followed policies that made the Maldives vulnerable to religious radicalism. During his rule, in 1994, the Protection for Religious Unity Act was passed which restricted freedom to practise any religion other than Islam. Gayoom constituted the Supreme Council for Islamic Affairs in 1996 which was given the responsibility to oversee religious affairs in the country. This was renamed as the Ministry of Islamic Affairs in 2008. This body of clerics put pressure on the Maldivian Government to carry out moral and cultural policing of alleged anti-Islamic activities. It asked police to ban celebrations on New Year's eve viewing them as contrary to Islam.

Gayoom introduced Arabic medium schools and replaced the liberal Islamic studies textbooks with a stricter version that was imported from the Gulf countries. Students who passed out from these Islamic schools went on to study in Islamic universities in Egypt, Saudi Arabia, and Pakistan. They returned to the Maldives with Saudi funds and started preaching a stricter version of Islam hitherto unknown in the country.

The new generation which is returning after completing their education from these places is no longer content with just preaching radical Islam, they are even resorting to violence. In Pakistan, seminaries like the Jamia Salafia Islamia at Faisalabad have produced several Al Qaeda and Lashkar-e-Taiba leaders. Maldivians who have studied at such places are also getting drawn into jihadi networks.

Gayoom when in power however managed to control Islamist extremism as he took steps against extremist religious preachers. He banned women wearing veils on grounds of security. Still, situation started to deteriorate towards the end of his regime.

Emergence of Extremist Organisations

As a result of the policies of Gayoom and the social processes that took place in the 1970s, a number of Islamist extremist organisations have now come up in the Maldives. In the political arena the most prominent organisation is the Adhaalath Party (Justice Party). Gayoom was educated at Cairo's Al-Azhar seminary and his worldview was probably also coloured by the 1979 Islamic Revolution of Iran. In 1998, he enacted a constitution that gave him "the ultimate authority to impart the tenets of Islam" but his religious authority was questioned by Islamic groups. Gayoom's crackdown on these religious groups gave birth to the Adhaalath Party.[17] However, there are a number of groups who are outside the parliament but are far more radical. One such group is Idara Khidmat-e-Khalq (IKK) which is a charitable front of Lashkar-e-Taiba. The IKK started its operation in the Maldives in the aftermath of Tsunami in 2004. It recruited a number of Maldivian youth and sent them to seminaries in Pakistan. The IKK played an important role in increasing the involvement of the Maldivian youth in the global jihadi network.

Another prominent Islamist organisation, Jamiyyathul Salaf is registered as a non-governmental organisation (NGO) with the Ministry of Home Affairs. Its stated objective is to "raise religious awareness and promote the values of Islam". This group is actively engaged in spreading Salafi Islam in the Maldives. In 2008, it declared music to be haram (forbidden) and forced a school library in Malé to close down as it had "Christian story books". It also invited a preacher, Bilal Philips in 2009, who endorsed marrying off Muslim girls as soon as they attained puberty.

Involvement of Maldivians in Terror Attacks

The increasing Islamic radicalism in the country has led to involvement of Maldivians in terror attacks both inside the country as well as outside. The first terror attack in the Maldives took place in September 2007 when a bomb blast injured 12 foreign tourists in the Sultan Park in Malé. During this time, the pro-democracy movement was at its height, and the attack was initially seen as an effort to upset the arrival of foreign tourists in the Maldives, which has remained a major source of national income and revenue for the government. Subsequently, however three Maldivian men were arrested who confessed that they had carried out the blasts with the objective to "target, attack and injure non-Muslims" as part of (global) jihad. The law enforcement agencies of the Maldives carried out a related raid on a mosque in the Itimadoo Island which was resisted by the Islamists and the Maldivian National Defence Force (MNDF) had to be called in.[18]

At least two Maldivians are known to have died fighting in Kashmir in early 2007. Nasheed had also pointed to "a Maldivian connection" to the terrorist attacks in Mumbai in 2008.

Since 2008 an increasing number of Maldivians have sought to travel to Pakistan for jihadist training. It is believed that some people involved in the Sultan Park bombing did it in exchange for travel from the islands after the operation in order to study at a madrassa in Pakistan.[19] International terrorist groups like the Lashkar-e-Taiba have also been trying to use the Maldives as a base.

A number of Maldivians have been arrested in terrorism-related activities or while they were trying to go to Pakistan for jihadi training. On April 2, 2009 the Maldivian Defence Ministry announced that nine armed Maldivians were arrested in the northern district of Waziristan, Pakistan.[20] Few days before, three Maldivians were arrested for illegally entering the Waziristan tribal area in Pakistan. However, it was not clearly established whether these Maldivians were on their way to join the Taliban or were planning an attack. One of those arrested was said be an accused in the Sultan Park explosion case, but was reportedly released earlier for want of evidence. One Maldivian national has spent three years at the Guantanamo US detention facility in Cuba. Ten Maldivians were still in Pakistani jails.

On 8 November, 2009, the Al Qaeda released a video clip which featured a Maldivian national who reportedly killed himself in a suicide attack. The person shown in the clipping was Ali Jaleel, a resident of Malé.

In recent years, the remote uninhabited islands of the Maldives have been a concern from the security point of view. It is feared that jihadis could use its remote islands as safe heavens. So far, neither Adhaalath nor Salaf have been linked with armed violence, but they do pose a threat to the Maldivian way of life. They however do not enjoy much popular support, and Adhaalath does not win too many seats in the parliamentary elections. They mostly get followers by either intimidation or labelling their critics as anti-Islam. Maldives at present may not have armed Islamist organisations, but there are terrorist cells operating in the country which could be mobilised when orders are received from headquarters in Pakistan, Afghanistan, or even India.[21]

Islamists in Post-Gayoom Era

The Islamists of Maldives were far more active under the democratic government of Nasheed than they ever were under Gayoom. The much talked about democratic reforms that had brought in a new constitution and multi-party elections in 2008 did not include religious freedom or religious reform.[22] Moreover, the ruling coalition of President Nasheed included Adhaalath Party, which has been described by many as an extremist group. It also controlled the Ministry of Islamic Affairs, as the Party had helped Nasheed in the run-up to the 2008 elections.

The appeasement of religious parties like Adhaalath by Nasheed under his democratic government allowed extremists to advocate their version of Islam without fear of being arrested and detained. They were able to operate and preach more freely and organise rallies. On the other hand, Gayoom used to jail religious extremists like the controversial preacher, Sheikh Farid.

It is also alleged that the participation of Adhaalath in Nasheed's coalition government gave the extremists a new legitimacy. They were in control of the Ministry of Islamic Affairs which allowed them to have far more influence on religious affairs than was warranted by the political clout they had in the country.

Initially, Adhaalath as part of the ruling coalition seemed useful as it allowed the government to deal easily with the more extreme Salafis on various religious issues. It was also believed that Adhaalath within government was far less dangerous than outside. It was feared that once outside the government, it might join hands with the Salafis.

Adhaalath however overtime became quite assertive. When President Nasheed tried to revise the penal code, he faced stiff opposition from a small but vocal section that wanted the sharia law punishments like death penalty, flogging, and amputations to be included. They even organised several demonstrations in favour of flogging and threatened those who opposed it.

Interestingly, in the Maldives, women enjoy greater economic and social empowerment in comparison to other South Asian countries. They have been described as the most emancipated in the Muslim world. Maldivian women have always kept their own name after marriage, and could remarry, inherit property, and mix freely with men.[23] Still, a certain contradiction can be seen in the approach of Maldivian society towards women. The prevailing law in the Maldives considers both pre-marital sex and adultery as offences punishable by flogging; it is particularly harsher for women.[24] In 2006, there were 184 cases of flogging in public for extra marital sex, of which 146 were women. As per the prevailing sharia law, abortion is considered a sin, and the Adhaalath Party in particular wanted execution of women who had aborted their foetuses.[25]

Adhaalath was also suspected of fuelling Islamic extremism because of its strong connections with Saudi Arabia. The free arrival of qualified and unqualified clerics from abroad worsened the problem of extremism. The Religious Affairs Minister banned former pop singer Al Rameez from reciting the azaan (call to prayer) and leading prayers in the mosques. He suspended Imam of Ibrahmi Mosque without valid reasons and blocked Islamic websites indiscriminately. There was also inconsistency in awarding preaching licences.

Most importantly, the Minister was opposed to opening to the public the tomb of Abdul Barakaa Yoosuf-al Barbari, at Medhu Ziyaaraiy, who is believed to have brought Islam in the Maldives in 1153 AD. The Adaalath party called it un-Islamic and forbidden by religion.

The entry of Tabligh Jamaat was banned during the regime of Gayoom under the provisions of "Protection of Religious Unity Act". Moreover, the guidelines regarding religious preaching stated that only scholars with an undergraduate degree from an Islamic university and who have lived in the Maldives for a minimum of one year were eligible for preaching. The Nasheed government however allowed a Tabligh delegation from Sri Lanka to visit the Maldives to preach in June 2009. This visit became controversial, but the Religious Affairs Minister defended the decision by saying that the members of the Tabligh were not extremists. Endorsement of such activities led to the emergence of various religious organisations which not only caused confusion of religious principles, but some of these organisations were also suspected to have links with foreign religious extremist groups.

The government also gave in to the demands of religious extremists when they objected to Airtel's TV Channel, God, which telecast round-the-clock preaching by Christian missionaries. The government asked Airtel to stop the telecast of this channel or face closure.

Nasheed's Government Admits Rising Extremism

Islamist radicalism was one of the major problems facing the Nasheed government; however, the government only gradually realised its rise and tried to come to grips with it. To check the misuse of power by the Adhaalath Party, Nasheed appointed Sheikh Mohamed Farook, a religious scholar of the MDP, as the Deputy Minister of Religious Affairs. The government officially admitted that many Maldivians were secretly collaborating with foreign militant organisations especially in Afghanistan and Pakistan and taking part in jihad. In his weekly radio broadcast on October 30, 2009 Nasheed admitted that 10 Maldivians had died fighting in South Waziristan. He also revealed that there were close to 100 Maldivian nationals in Waziristan and in the border region of Pakistan and Afghanistan. Besides, 100 more Maldivian nationals were suspected to have received military training in Pakistan to fight the jihadist war.

To improve the situation, Nasheed contemplated taking action in consultation with the security and defence agencies in the country. He advised parents not to send their children to Pakistan or even to India to study in madrassas. He feared that even students sent to Pakistani universities could be recruited for extremist activities.

The phenomenon of rising Islamic extremism was also confirmed by Ahmed Abdul Kareem who was with the Human Rights Commission of the Maldives (HRCM). He pointed out that prayers were now being conducted in non-designated places, and in many cases, girls were not being sent to schools. Children were not being vaccinated and girls were often forced to marry at a young age. Cases of concubinage were also reported. He criticised the government for not taking action against the extremist religious leaders and allowing them to spread religious fundamentalism in the Maldives.

Extremism Hampered Promotion of Tourism

To improve the economic situation of the country Nasheed wanted to promote tourism, the largest foreign exchange earner for the country. To achieve this objective it was necessary to relax strict Islamic laws. His attempts to provide better facilities for tourism however were thwarted by the assertion of the religious right and the judiciary. His government had allowed sale of alcohol in the inhabited islands. But on February 26, 2010 a coalition of NGOs held a large demonstration in Malé against this decision. Senior members of Adhaalath Party also participated in the demonstration and threatened to resign. This issue sparked a vigorous debate across the country and the new regulations were eventually withdrawn. Subsequently, Nasheed was also forced to roll back his plan of allowing more multinational companies to set up resorts on unutilised islands.

The Maldivian Government was also forced to briefly close all hotel spas and health centres in resort hotels in December 2011 after the Adhaalath Party alleged that these were fronts for prostitution. This decision was however reversed as the country critically depended on tourism.[26]

Gayoom had developed two worlds in the Maldives. Resorts were purposely kept away from the islands where Maldivian people were living. This to some extent had satisfied the orthodox people in the country.

The Unholy Alliance of Islamists and 'Democrats'

Nasheed faced problems from Islamist radicals mainly because he represented moderate Islam. The opposition-dominated parliament sought to impeach the then education minister, Musthafa Lufthy, in June 2010 after he proposed to make Islam and the national Dhivehi language optional, instead of mandatory, subjects in high schools.

The Islamist radicals even demolished the monument constructed by Pakistan at Addu city on the occasion of the 17th South Asian Association of Regional Cooperation (SAARC) summit in November 2011 which showcased Pakistan's pluralistic heritage.[27] The opposition accused Nasheed of being a friend of Israel and the Christian West and of undermining Islam. The hardliners opposed Nasheed's restoration of diplomatic relations with Israel. They also wanted the government to stop Israeli flights and tourists from coming to the Maldives. Nasheed was considered close to Conservative Party of Britain, which has had long-standing links with President Nasheed's MDP, and several Tory officials have worked for him as advisors.[28]

Nasheed believed that freedom of expression was sacrosanct, and hence he did not impose any restriction on the increasingly extremist and hardline rhetoric of the Islamists. When concerned liberals approached Nasheed, he wanted them to act on their own to check extremists. But the extremist movement by now became too strong for individuals to contain without any state support. Moreover, the extremists used the labels of apostasy, heresy, and anti-Islamic agent to discredit any liberal effort.

The Adhaalath Party created a motley group of religious NGOs and anti-Nasheed political parties in what came to be known as the Maldives National Movement (MNM). One of the sub-plans of MNM was the 'December 23 movement', which also played a role in the ouster of Nasheed on February 7, 2012. This was also a case of domestic forces hostile to a legitimate regime in a small state becoming unmanageable and leading to a change of regime.[29]

Islamists despite their influence on a section of population would not have been able to depose Nasheed on their own. But many opposition parties came together and used the 'threat to Islam' for opportunistic purposes. In the December 23, 2011 protests, eight opposition parties and allied NGOs participated. This alliance also included a number of resort owners as well as individuals who in the past had spoken against rising extremism in the country. Prominent among them was Dr. Hasan Saeed who had co-authored a book, *Freedom of Religion, Apostasy and Islam.* Former president Gayoom also had a statement read out in favour of protests.

The DQP published a pamphlet that had the alleged details of a secret agenda pursued by Nasheed to undermine Maldivian Islamic faith. Nasheed government's decision to foster business with Israel was seen as an 'alliance with Jews' and his bilateral ties with Western governments was portrayed as friendship with 'enemies of Islam'. Misusing freedom of expression, it sought to convince Maldivians that modernity and Islam are diametrically opposed to each other. It equated overthrow of Nasheed's government with religious duty.

Thus, the concerted efforts of Islamists and some of the mainstream parties ensured the ouster of Nasheed.

Nasheed's Lack of Political Abilities

Nasheed is by nature an activist and not a shrewd politician. It was unwise of him to allow the parliament to be controlled by the opposition. His party remained in minority. This situation emerged because Nasheed did not care to take along his allies whose support was crucial for his victory in the presidential elections. In contrast, Gayoom-led DRP managed to get a simple majority in Maldivian parliament with the help of PA and some independents.

Under the Maldives' system of government, the president handpicks his cabinet and each nomination must be approved by the parliament. The parliament also has the power to remove a minister through a no-confidence vote. Though the DRP gained control of the legislature, it fell short of a two-thirds majority which would have enabled it to even impeach the president. At the same time, Nasheed had no power to dismiss the assembly until it completed its full five-year term. The outcome of this system was such that Nasheed's government was hamstrung, and the country could not avert a political crisis.

Some of the opposition parties of Maldives were not happy with the education minister of the the Nasheed government for his liberal views. To remove him from his post, the opposition-controlled parliament planned to bring a no-confidence motion against him. The cabinet however pre-empted the move by resigning en-masse on June 28, 2010. This decision also triggered a political crisis in the Maldives and left the country without any government for two weeks. The government claimed that opposition MPs were not allowing the executive to function properly and were making it impossible for ministers to discharge their constitutional duties. The same day police arrested three key opposition MPs for allegedly bribing parliamentarians with cash to vote against the government. This decision worsened the crisis.

The en-masse resigning of the Nasheed's team was a major mistake. This also showed his political immaturity. He thought that this dramatic action would shock the parliament and make them fall in line. Unfortunately, it led to a completely different scenario. Now to restore his team, they had to be approved by the parliament which was controlled by the opposition. As a result, some important ministers whom the opposition did not like were not approved. The government argued that parliamentary consent was 'ceremonial'. However, the Supreme Court ruled on December 10, 2010 that the rejected ministers could not remain in their positions. Nasheed accepted the decision as the way forward for establishing constitutional democracy.

The opposition also tried to stop the privatisation of the Malé International Airport on nationalistic grounds and alleged corruption in the deal. One of the main reasons for some key opposition members to oppose the government's privatization of the Malé airport was because they were business tycoons and had benefitted from the earlier system. Hasan Sayeed, leader of the DQP, was allegedly receiving huge legal fees from two MPs, Yameen and Gasim.

President Naseed attributed this political crisis in the Maldives to the constitution. The constitution adopted on August 7, 2008 is based on a presidential system of governance. But it has wider powers vested with the parliament, aimed at maintaining necessary checks and balances. This system becomes problematic in case the parliament is controlled by the opposition, as was the case then. It allowed the opposition to obstruct the core functions of the executive, such as raising taxes and providing subsidies.

Nasheed was of the view that only an amendment to the constitution would bring political stability in the country. He also considered changing the Maldivian political system into a parliamentary system by seeking immediate re-election. Some laws passed in the parliament made it difficult for him to play the role of the executive according to the constitution. He wanted this to be rectified.

The government and the opposition also tried to sort out the issue by mutual dialogue without international mediation. To facilitate talks, Nasheed released the opposition leader, Yameen. In an attempt to reach out to the opposition he congratulated the opposition party DRP on its fifth anniversary. He also expressed confidence that the DRP would cooperate with the government in its efforts to find an amicable solution to the political impasse in the Maldives.

Unfortunately, not everyone in the Maldives was looking for a solution to the political crisis. In fact, a section of the DRP MPs declared that they would forward a no-confidence motion against President Mohamed Nasheed for violating the constitution.

There was some hope of overcoming this political crisis when Gayoom's party DRP split. Gayoom meanwhile formed another political party, the Progressive Party of Maldives (PPM).[30] A shrewd politician would have attempted to gain majority in this situation by approaching the splinter group. Nasheed unfortunately did not try to expand his alliance. On the contrary, his ham-handedness only allowed all political parties, except the MDP, to be on the same page.

The Maldives during this period faced the threat of civil strife, and there were several clashes between Nasheed supporters and the security forces. The situation was precipitated by the politically naïve Nasheed. His lack of political acumen allowed parliament to be controlled by the opposition, and he tried to take on all political adversaries even when he himself was politically weak. Things really worsened when he tried to go after Gayoom, who was after all was still the most powerful person in the Maldives.

Mishandling of the Political Crisis by Nasheed

Maldives was plunged into a deep political crisis when Nasheed ordered the arrest of the Chief Criminal Judge, Abdulla Mohamed, in a joint operation of Police and the MNDF on the January 16, 2012. The judge had ordered the release of a government critic and opposition leader, Mohamed Jameel Ahmed, who according to him was illegally detained. The arrested person had allegedly defamed the government during a television interview in which he accused Nasheed's government of working against the state religion, Islam, with the support of Christians and Jews.

Ironically, Islamic radicalism had grown after Nasheed came to power. The prevailing democracy in the country provided them a lot of space. The government thought that the liberal atmosphere in the country would allow Islamists to come out in open and they could then be engaged and countered politically.[31] But the MDP government underestimated their strength, and the Islamists created great difficulty for the government.

Nasheed's order to have judge Abdulla Mohamed arrested on January 16, 2012 provided an opportunity to marry Nasheed's alleged anti-Islamic activities with his violation of the constitution. The opposition used it for political opportunism.

There was no doubt that the judiciary in Maldives was in a mess. A large number of unqualified and incompetent people had come into the judiciary towards the end of Gayoom's dictatorship. But the public in general disapproved the arrest of Judge Abdullah. The Supreme Court of Maldives passed an order for his immediate release. Even this order was ignored by the Nasheed government, alienating some conscientious lawyers leading to the resignation of the SAARC's first woman Secretary General, Fathimath Dhiyana Saeed. She joined the protestors along with her husband.

It also created confusion in the country, and rumours started circulating that Nasheed wanted to fill the judiciary with his people. Due to the mishandling of the situation, a political stand-off with religious overtones was transformed into an impasse between his government and the judiciary, which prompted many of his supporters to desert him. It precipitated the crisis resulting in his ouster. This struggle between institutions also provided a chance to the remnants of dictatorship to assert itself and discredit the first democratically elected government in the Maldives.

Political Transition or Coup

A section of people in Maldives as well as in international community described the resignation of Nasheed as a coup. Nasheed's own party, the MDP alleged that the resignation had been engineered by "rogue elements" of the police and military, along with supporters of former president Maumoon Abdul Gayoom. The MDP also alleged that the opposition threatened the president with a bloodbath if he refused to resign. Nasheed also stated in his televised address that he chose to resign to protect the public from further violence.

The Maldivian Islamists played an instrumental role in the events of February 7, 2012 which led to the exit of first democratically elected president of the Maldives. The Islamists thought that they had performed a 'religious duty' by facilitating the removal from power of Nasheed who in their view was an anti-Islamic heretic.

A day after the removal of Nasheed, the Adhaalath Party put out a press release in which it called the people to stand up against Nasheed 'with swords and guns' and any Maldivian who failed to do so was a sinner and had no right to live in the country. They also said that accepting Waheed as 'a just ruler' was a religious duty of the Maldivian Muslims. The same day, the extremists destroyed the Buddhist relics kept in a museum in Malé.

Waheed was not ideologically aligned to the Adhaalath Party. Adhaalath supported Waheed because he had not openly sided with Nasheed in his many stand-offs with the extremists. However, this was because Nasheed did not allow him to participate in any decision that mattered. This was also one of the major reasons of unhappiness of Waheed with Nasheed.

Fumbling of Indian Diplomacy

The political crisis in Maldives found Indian diplomacy wanting. Nasheed claimed to be a friend of India and also claimed to follow an India first policy. During his regime the cooperation between the Indian Army and the MNDF also deepened further.

There were indications that Nasheed and his party wanted India to intervene militarily during the Maldivian political crisis as it once had during the 1988 crisis. But the situation this time was starkly different from what it was during the Gayoom era. At that time Indian forces were sent to help the Gayoom regime against an incursion by the PLOTE, a Tamil militant group from Sri Lanka. But in the political crisis of February 2012 both the parties were from Maldives. In this situation, it would not have been prudent of the Indian Government to take sides. However, India could have acted at an earlier stage and pre-empted the crisis.

Nasheed was also disappointed by the quick recognition of the Waheed regime by India. Countries like the US too recognised the Waheed government, but they had different game plan. They thought they would use the new regime for their own purposes.

Setback to Multi-party Democracy

The first democratically elected government could not last its full term in the Maldives. This was a definite setback to democracy. However, the democratic experiment in Maldives was a new phenomenon, and hence some teething problems were to be expected. The Nasheed government faced problems because in the Maldivian system of governance there is division of power between the president and the parliament. To run the country smoothly the party of the president in power needs to control the parliament as well, in the absence of which the opposition could create hindrance in governance. This is exactly what happened when Nasheed was the president.

Nasheed's popularity in the Maldives started waning as he struggled to deliver the political and economic reforms he promised in the face of parliamentary resistance. The multi-party democracy also faced problems partly because the country at that time was in the grip of serious economic crisis.

The aim of Nasheed was to bring an exemplary democratic system to the Maldives which could serve as a model for other Muslim countries in the region. For this, the Maldives needed to manage its modernisation, liberal democracy, and Islam, all together. It was hoped that Nasheed would be able to do that. However, the problem of Islamic fundamentalism in the Maldives proved to be serious one and the unceremonious exit of Nasheed made the peaceful transition to multi-party democracy uncertain.

NOTES

1. Nicholas Milton, "Maldives Holds First Fully Democratic Parliamentary Election," *The Telegraph*, London, May 8, 2009, at http://www.telegraph.co.uk/news/worldnews/africaandindianocean/maldives/5297813/Maldives-holds-first-fully-democratic-parliamentary-election.html.
2. Maryam Omidi, "Provisional Results Reveal Opposition Victory", *Minivan News*, May 13, 2009, at http://www.minivannews.com/news_detail.php?id=6509.
3. "Foreign Minister Dr. Ahmed Shaheed Joins the Ruling Maldivian Democratic Party," High Commission of the Republic of Maldives in the United Kingdom of Great Britain and Northern Ireland, October 5, 2009, at http://www.maldiveshighcommission.org/archive/?s=10&grupa=3&id=1333&new=ok.
4. Roland Buerk, "Maldives Adopt New Constitution", BBC News, August 7, 2007, at http://news.bbc.co.uk/2/hi/south_asia/7547725.stm (Accessed August 16, 2015).
5. Dr. Hassan Saeed and Dr Ahmed Shaheed, "Democratic Transition in the Maldives," *South Asian Journal*, p. 54.
6. J J Robinson, "Police on Defense over DhiFM Coverage of Muleeage Mob," *Minivan News*, January 30, 2010, at http://minivannews.com/politics/police-on-defense-over-dhifm-coverage-of-muleeage-mob-2967.
7. Hilath Rasheed, "Maldives in 2010: Birth Pangs of a Democracy," *South Asian Journal*, p. 131.
8. Ahmed Naish, "Decentralisation Bill Passed as MDP MPs Walk out," Minivan News, April 28, 2010, at http://minivannews.com/politics/decentralisation-bill-passed-as-mdp-mps-walk-out-6444.
9. "JSC's Re-Appointment of Judges outside Constitutional Provisions Remains a 'Huge Challenge' – President Nasheed," The President's Office, Republic of Maldives, January 27, 2012, at http://www.presidencymaldives.gov.mv/?lid=11&dcid=6659; Also see: Aishath Velezinee, "Comment: Appointment of Supreme Court Bench a Grave Blunder," March 27, 2013, at http://minivannews.com/politics/comment-appointment-of-supreme-court-bench-a-grave-blunder-55248.
10. Hilath Rasheed, No. 7, p. 129.
11. Based on author's interview during a recent field visit to Maldives.
12. Based on interviews conducted during the field visit.
13. Hassan Ahmed Maniku, "Conversion of Maldives to Islam," *Journal of the Royal Asiatic Society*, 31 (87), 1986, p. 79.

14. Patrick Roberts, "Trouble in Paradise: Islamist Radicalism in the Maldives," *Jane's Intelligence Review*, May 2011, p. 15.
15. Tufail Ahmad, "Bombers from the Maldives," *The New Indian Express*, July 17, 2014, at http://www.newindianexpress.com/columns/2014/07/17/Bombers-from-the-Maldives/article2333778.ece, (Accessed August 19, 2015).
16. Roshni Thomas, "Radicalism in the Maldives: Should India be worried?," Institute for Peace and Conflict Studies, June 15, 2015, at http://www.ipcs.org/article/terrorism/radicalism-in-the-maldives-should-india-be-worried-4888.html.
17. Tufail Ahmad, No. 15.
18. N Sathiya Moorthy, "Maldives: Islam, Nationalism and 'Islamic Nationalism'," Observer Research Foundation, 11, June 2013, at http://orfonline.org/cms/sites/orfonline/modules/analysis/AnalysisDetail.html?cmaid=52941&mmacmaid=52942.
19. Patrick Roberts, No. 14, p. 16.
20. "Pakistani's Security Force Arrest 9 Armed Maldivians," Maldives National Defence Force, April 1, 2009, at http://www.mndf.gov.mv/news.asp.
21. Sudha Ramachandran, "Maldives Faces up to Extremism," *Asia Times online*, November 11, 2009, at http://www.atimes.com/atimes/South_Asia/KK11Df02.html.
22. N Sathiya Moorthy, No. 18.
23. A.M. Shaljan, "Population, Gender and Development in Maldives," *Economic & Political Weekly*, 39 (18), May 1-7, 2004, p. 1838.
24. Ankita Shree, "Maldives: Women, Abortion and Politics," October 5, 2011, *Mainstream*, XLIX (41), October 1, 2011.
25. Ibid.
26. Jethro Mullen, "Maldives Reverses Spa Ban," *CNN*, January 4, 2012, at http://edition.cnn.com/2012/01/04/world/asia/maldives-spas-ruling/.
27. Ahmed Naish, "Pakistan's 'Idolatrous' SAARC Monument Set Ablaze by Protesters," *Minivan News*, November 14, 2011, at http://minivannews.com/society/pakistans-idolatrous-saarc-monument-set-ablaze-by-protesters-28172.
28. Dean Nelson, "Ex-Maldives President: I May Be Facing 40 Charges," *The Telegraph*, London, February 9, 2012, at http://www.telegraph.co.uk/news/worldnews/africaandindianocean/maldives/9071193/Ex-Maldives-president-I-may-be-facing-40-charges.html.
29. Jonathan Alford, "Security Dilemmas of a Small State," *The World Today*, Royal Institute of International Affairs, 40 (8/9), August-September 1984, p. 368.
30. "Ex President Gayoom Quits DRP to Form New Party," *Asian Tribune*, September 5, 2011, at http://www.asiantribune.com/news/2011/09/04/ex-president-gayoom-quits-drp-form-new-party; also see: Ahmed Naish, "Gayoom's New Party to be Called Progressive Party of Maldives," *Minivan News*, September 5, 2011, at http://minivannews.com/politics/gayooms-new-party-to-be-called-progressive-party-of-maldives-25076.
31. Based on the author's interview with the Special Envoy to President Nasheed.

4

MALDIVES UNDER WAHEED

After the resignation of Mohamed Nasheed as the president, the Vice President, Dr. Mohamed Waheed Hassan Manik was elevated to the position of the president. The changeover however failed to bring political stability to the country especially as Nasheed claimed that he was made to resign at gunpoint.

Subsequent enquiry commissions absolved Waheed of any wrongdoing, but the political developments afterwards indicated otherwise. Waheed after taking over as president immediately released judge Abduallah, but afterwards there was no move to investigate the charges against him. Waheed promised a national government of all political parties, but all the seven members initially included in his government were former Gayoom loyalists. Gayoom's daughter, Dhuniya, was made State Foreign Minister. The support of Islamists to Waheed earned them a place in his government. The leader of the DQP, Mohmed Jameel was made home minister in Waheed's government. Dr. Hasan Saeed was appointed as President Waheed's special advisor. The MDP, Nasheed's party, decided not to join the government, and Nasheed, fearing arrest, took shelter in the Indian High Commission on February 13, 2013.

Nasheed was seen as a front-runner for the presidential elections that were expected in November 2013. His opponents however wanted him to be convicted for 'the unconstitutional arrest of Judge Abdulla.' This would have made Nasheed ineligible for contesting the upcoming presidential elections. Nasheed however came out of the Indian High Commission on February 23, 2013 after an understanding was reached with the Maldivian government that he would not be arrested again and allowed to contest the presidential elections. During negotiations with the Waheed government India conveyed that its "interest was only in a free, fair, credible and inclusive election."[1]

The GMR Controversy

Maldives under Nasheed had signed an agreement in 2010 with the GMR-led consortium for upgrading and running of the Malé international airport. This deal however started unravelling after a local court struck down the deal's provisions allowing the operator (GMR) to charge a $ 25 airport development fee and $ 2 insurance surcharge as illegal on December 8, 2011. The court verdict dramatically altered the finances of the deal. The Nasheed government however then gave assurance that the company's commercial interests would be protected and the loss of revenue adjusted against the revenue due to the state by way of payments to the Maldives Airport Company Ltd (MACL).[2]

The GMR Group did not appeal against the court verdict thinking that the assurance of the government was sufficient to take care of its interests. However, the assurance came to naught once Nasheed was deposed and in his place Waheed came to power. GMR had not taken political risk insurance and relied completely on the then state of relationship between India and the Maldives. Subsequently, it also turned out that the amount GMR was to get from the government dwarfed the concession fee that the government would receive from the airport's operator.

To make the agreement somewhat palatable, GMR offered to waive the Airport Development Fee (ADF) for Maldivian nationals. It also refuted the charge that the company was replacing Maldivian workers with cheap Indian labour. It was pointed out that the number of Maldivians who held jobs at the airport had gone up from 1,483 at the time of the takeover to 1,663. The company asserted that the deal was entered into after a transparent global tender and the consortium had delivered their side of the bargain. Moreover, the Maldives Anti-Corruption Commission in its report in 2010 had found no fault with the bidding process.

President Waheed however claimed that GMR was misled by the previous Nasheed government into signing a legally unsustainable agreement.[3] He also blamed GMR for not willing to renegotiate the terms of the agreement. The Waheed government declared the agreement 'void ab initio' on November 28, 2012.[4]

The GMR Group moved the Singapore High Court against the Maldivian Government's decision. According to the project contract, in case of any difference between the parties, the law of either Singapore or the UK would apply. In response to the GMR petition, Singapore High Court granted injunctive relief against the termination of the contract.[5] However, the Maldives hardened its stand and said that its termination decision was "non-reversible and non-negotiable" and said no such injunction can be issued against a sovereign state. The GMR Group demanded $ 800 million in compensation. This arbitration finally went in favour of GMR.

On 23 February 2016 the arbitration tribunal in Singapore ruled in favour of the GMR group of companies on its dispute with the Maldives Government on the airport project in that country. The tribunal decided that GMR was entitled to payment of damages for termination of its contract in Maldives for the airport, including all the money GMR had borrowed from Axis Bank for the project.[6] On June 18, 2014, in its first order, the tribunal had also ruled that the original concession agreement was valid and binding and that the Maldives Government and Maldives Airports Company Limited (MACL) had unlawfully scrapped the same. It held them jointly liable to pay damages.[7] The Axis Bank leads a consortium of lenders, which includes Indian Overseas Bank and Indian Bank, with exposure to the airport project. The Maldivian Government however still insists that it would fight the Rf 160 million claimed by GMR, and that GMR has to prove the exact amount spent on the airport.[8]

The GMR issue damaged the bilateral India-Maldives relationship. India decided to freeze aid to the 'politically unstable' Maldives. The Indian media continued with the narrative that the Maldives faced the danger of takeover by Al Qaeda or elements sympathetic to Al Qaeda because of its shallow democratic roots, highly competitive elite and dispersed population. India also considered the Waheed government in Malé as an interim and unrepresentative government. Under the prevailing circumstances, India was unsure whether the funds meant for normal development activities would be put to the purpose they were meant for.[9]

The lack of a government policy regarding the engagement of its corporate sector in foreign countries created an awkward situation for India. There is no unanimity whether the government should intervene in such cases. The Indian Government does not and cannot control private companies' behaviour overseas. Unlike the United States, India does not have an anti-foreign bribery law. Moreover, India's record on corporate corruption is quite poor. Thus, the government involvement on behalf of an Indian corporate would hold India's image and foreign policy hostage to poor corporate behaviour. Even if the corporate is well-behaved, someone in the government would have to take a call to deploy state capabilities in its defence in case of need. Then in that case the government might face the charge of crony capitalism.[10] Therefore, it is much better for the corporates to assess political risks themselves and take their investment decisions.

However, the award of contract to GMR to upgrade and run Malé airport should not be seen as purely a commercial venture from India's perspective. GMR was allowed to run the main airport of the Maldives which is its only gateway. In this sense, it was not only the most profitable project for the company but also a big strategic advantage to India. Hence, it should have been carefully handled and its financial aspect should have been closely monitored. But all the advantages were lost because of the mishandling of the whole affair.

Moreover, a section of politicians in the Maldives managed to stir opposition to this project. For example, as mentioned earlier, politicians like Yameen and Gasim Ibrahim, who had the contract to supply fuel, opposed the project as they had benefitted personally from the earlier system. Their lawyer, Hasan Sayeed of the DQM, was alienated by Nasheed leading to him leaving the ruling coalition. Subsequently, the GMR project was also opposed by the Islamists.

Further, though Waheed's government was simply a stopgap – he was in power just because the government of Nasheed could not complete its full term, he used his anti-India sentiment, which was evident right from the start of his term, to good effect. Waheed used the GMR contract controversy to build himself up as a credible presidential candidate for the 2013 elections by challenging the regional power, India.[11]

Indian Approach to Political Crisis in Maldives

India was quite prompt in recognising Waheed's government in the Maldives. However, Waheed didn't reciprocate the gesture. His anti-India approach and his friendliness to China were only too obvious. Political instability in the Maldives was not in the interest of India. Still, instead of taking a pro-active approach, the Indian Government decided to allow the internal process to sort out the issues that were thrown up by the transfer of power from the former President, Mohamed Nasheed, to the new President, Waheed Hassan Manik. It also wanted them to agree on an election date. This approach found wide acceptance among countries such as the US and Sri Lanka that have a strong interest in the Maldives.[12]

In India, after the removal of Nasheed there was concern that Islamists might gain ground in the Maldives. It was also feared that the situation of political vacuum would be used by Islamists to harm democracy in the Maldives. However, it appears that Waheed had tied up with the Islamists only for tactical reasons. Waheed had himself worked in the United Nations and his western educated children are not considered extremists. In fact, it was found later that the US tried to use this Indian campaign gainst possible rise of extremism in the Maldives to promote its own strategic interests in that country. The Indian influence in the Maldives suffered during Waheed's regime because of the misreading of Waheed and his allegiance to China and probably also to the US.

NOTES

1. R.K. Radhakrishnan, "Nasheed leaves Indian embassy after 'deal'," *The Hindu*, February 23, 2013, at http://www.thehindu.com/news/international/south-asia/nasheed-leaves-indian-embassy-after-deal/article4446333.ece
2. K K Sruthijith, "GMR Spat: Maldives Ends Deal after Waiting 45 Days for PM Manmohan Singh; Wanted to Explain Why Deal was Unsustainable," *The Economic Times*, December 6, 2012, at http://articles.economictimes.indiatimes.com/2012-12-

06/news/35647680_1_masood-imad-Malé-international-airport-sidharath-kapur (Accessed August 16, 2015).

3. Interview of President Waheed, "The GMR Case Shows Our No-nonsense Approach," Rediff.com, December 8,2012, at http://www.rediff.com/business/interview/interview-gmr-case-shows-our-no-nonsense-approach/20121208.htm (Accessed August 16, 2015).
4. J.J. Robinson, "Maldives cancels GMR's $511 million airport project," *Reuters*, Nov 28, 2012, at http://in.reuters.com/article/maldives-india-gmr-idINDEE8AR01Z 20121128
5. T.E. Narasimhan, "Malé Was a Learning Experience: G M Rao," *Business Standard*, December5, 2012, at http://www.business-standard.com/article/companies/Malé-was-a-learning-experience-g-m-rao-112120500196_1.html .
6. "GMR Awarded Damages in Maldives Airport Arbitration Infra Giant to Also Get Compensation for Project Loan from Axis Bank," *Business Standard*, Mumbai, February 25, 2016, at http://www.business-standard.com/article/companies/gmr-awarded-damages-in-maldives-airport-arbitration-116022400818_1.html.
7. V Rishi Kumar, "Axis Bank Debt: GMR Infra Gets Favourable Order from Maldives Airport Tribunal," *The Hindu Businessline*, February 24, 2016, at http://www.thehindubusinessline.com/companies/gmr-infra-secures-favourable-order-from-arbitral-tribunal-on-axis-bank-debt/article8275804.ece.
8. Mohamed Visham, "Tribunal Finds Maldives Liable for Axis Bank Loan to GMR," *Haveeru Online*, February 24, 2016, at http://www.haveeru.com.mv/news/66794.
9. Aditi Phadnis, "India May Freeze Aid to 'Unstable Maldives,'" *Business Standard*, December 4, 2012, at http://www.business-standard.com/article/economy-policy/india-may-freeze-aid-to-unstable-maldives-112120402022_1.html (Accessed August 16, 2015).
10. "A Classic MNC Problem: GMR-Maldives Dispute Raises Difficult Questions for India," *Business Standard*, December 4, 2012, at http://www.business-standard.com/article/opinion/a-classic-mnc-problem-112120400193_1.html (Accessed August 16, 2015).
11. Jyoti Malhotra, "GMR Ouster a big blow to India's Reputation in S Asia," *Business Standard*, December 10, 2012, at http://www.business-standard.com/article/companies/gmr-ouster-a-big-blow-to-india-s-reputation-in-s-asia-112121000145_1.html (Accessed August 16, 2015).
12. R.K. Radhakrishnan, "Wide Acceptance for India's Stance on Maldives," *The Hindu*, February 21, 2012, at http://www.thehindu.com/news/international/article2913789.ece?css=print.

5

The Controversial Second Multi-party Elections

The Vice President Mohammed Waheed took over the reins of power in the Maldives after the crisis of February 7, 2012, and promised to uphold rule of law. However, a question mark over his government's legitimacy still remained. The deposed president, Nasheed kept demanding an early presidential election. On the other hand, President Waheed preferred an election once the situation stabilised. Nevertheless, continuous protests and demonstrations by the MDP and its leader, Nasheed, along with increasing pressure by the international community forced Waheed to go for the presidential elections a few months ahead of schedule, the first round (later annulled) was held on September 7, 2013. But the way elections were subsequently conducted, the Maldives could get a new government only few days after the end of Waheed's tenure, after November 11, 2013.

The Maldives witnessed a prolonged election process from September to November 2013 to elect a new president. In these elections, Abdulla Yameen, finally, emerged as the new president. His alliance also received a majority in the subsequent parliamentary elections that were held on March 22, 2014. Both these elections however were embroiled in controversy; still, Yameen was able to get a control over the parliament that provided him an opportunity to run the government smoothly.

Ironically, this has also made the future of multi-party democracy in the Maldives uncertain.

The 2013 Presidential Elections

The presidential elections were first scheduled for September 7, 2013. Waheed and his friends tried to stop Nasheed from contesting by implicating him in the court case related to the arrest of judge Abdullah. The game plan was that Nasheed's conviction would automatically bar him from contesting in elections.[1] However, under pressure from India and the international community it was agreed that the court would go slow on the case and Nasheed would be allowed to participate.

There were four main contenders in the presidential polls. Nasheed, the MDP's candidate was the strongest, followed by Abdulla Yameen of the PPM. The PPM, as mentioned in earlier, was a new political party formed by the former dictator, Gayoom, in October 2011, after he split from his earlier party, the DRP, which was headed by Ahmed Tasmeen Ali who had allied himself with the incumbent president, Waheed. President Waheed had formed a rainbow coalition, 'Forward with the Nation', which initially also included the fundamentalist Adhaalath Party. Adhaalath however dumped Waheed when he accused the party of having "extremist" individuals.[2] Subsequently, the Adhaalath Party supported another important candidate, the business tycoon Gasim Ibrahim, who was the Jumhooree Party (JP) candidate.

In the first round of elections that were held on September 7, 2013, Maldivian voters came out in large numbers and 88 per cent of the votes were polled. Nasheed emerged as the leading candidate and got 45.5 per cent of the votes polled. This, however, denied him outright victory, for which 50 per cent of the votes polled plus one more vote was required. Yameen received 25.35 per cent, while the share of Gasim Ibrahim was 24.07 per cent. Waheed received 5.13 per cent, which was the lowest vote share received by an incumbent president.

The first round of elections clearly indicated that the regime headed by Waheed was not a popular one, though earlier a Commonwealth-led probe had stated that the succession of Waheed was according to the constitution. The Commission of National Inquiry set up by the Maldivian Government in 2012, too, had found no evidence of a coup.

The run-off scheduled for September 28, 2013, however could not be held as Gasim Ibrahim went to the court challenging the validity of the elections. Subsequent developments indicated the weakness of democratic institutions in the Maldives and their misuse for electoral benefits by the influential candidates.

Tables 4, 5, and 6 show the official results for the annulled first, re-polled first, and second rounds of 2013 presidential elections, respectively.

Table 4: Official Result for the (annulled) First Round of Presidential Elections Held on September 7, 2013

#	*Full Name*	*Permanent Address*	*Political Party*	*Votes Received*	*Percentage*
1	Gasim Ibrahim	M. Maafannu Villa, Malé	JP	50,422	24.07
2	Mohamed Waheed Hassan	MA. Ureka, Malé	Independent	10,750	5.13
3	Abdulla Yameen Abdul Gayyoom	MA. Kaaminee Hulhanguge, Malé	PPM	53,099	25.35
4	Mohamed Nasheed	G. Kenereege, Malé	MDP	95,224	45.45
	Total valid votes			209,495	
	Total invalid votes			2,395	
	Total votes			211,890	
	Total number of eligible voters			239,593	

Source: Elections Commission, Republic of Maldives, at http://www.elections.gov.mv/presidentialelectionsresults2013.html.

Table 5: Official Result for the First Round of Presidential Elections Held on November 9, 2013

#	*Full Name*	*Permanent Address*	*Political Party*	*Votes Received*	*Percentage*
1	Gasim Ibrahim	M. Maafannu Villa, Malé	JP	48,131	23.34
3	Abdulla Yameen Abdul Gayyoom	MA. Kaaminee Hulhanguge, Malé	PPM	61,278	29.72
4	Mohamed Nasheed	G. Kenereege, Malé	MDP	96,764	46.93
	Total valid votes			206,173	
	Total invalid votes			2,331	
	Total votes			208,504	
	Total number of eligible voters			239,105	

Source: Elections Commission Republic of Maldives, at http://www.elections.gov.mv/presidentialelectionsresults2013.html.

Table 6: Official Result for the Second Round of Presidential Elections Held on November 16, 2013

#	*Full Name*	*Permanent Address*	*Political Party*	*Votes Received*	*Percentage*
3	Abdulla Yameen Abdul Gayyoom	MA. Kaaminee Hulhanguge, Malé	PPM	111,203	51.39
4	Mohamed Nasheed	G. Kenereege, Malé	MDP	105,181	48.61
	Total valid votes			216,384	
	Total invalid votes			2,237	
	Total votes			218,621	
	Total number of eligible voters			239,165	

Source: Elections Commission Republic of Maldives, at http://www.elections.gov.mv/presidentialelectionsresults2013.html.

Use of Institutions to Further Political and Electoral Interests

The 2013 presidential elections and the subsequent parliamentary elections in the Maldives clearly indicated that democratic institutions of the country were used to further political and electoral interests of the rich and powerful. As expected in the first round of presidential elections that were held on September 7, 2013, no clear winner emerged. Nasheed, despite his huge lead, could not go past 50 per cent of the votes polled. Abdulla Yameen and Gasim Ibrahim who were second and third-ranking candidates received even lesser votes.

For Gasim Ibrahim who came third with less than 3,000 votes, it meant that he could not have participated in the presidential run-off. The narrow margin of defeat made it further difficult for him to accept this situation. He petitioned the Supreme Court with allegations of electoral fraud in the first round. He also questioned electoral conduct in his rallies and on his television station, Villa TV. His main allegation was that the voter list was flawed and that in a properly held election he could have easily received more votes, and could have even been the leading candidate.

In this endeavour, Gasim Ibrahim was also supported by Yameen. Yameen could not have hoped to become president in the run-off without the support of Gasim Ibrahim's Jumhooree Party. This situation was quite similar to 2008 when Gayoom had received nearly 48 per cent of votes, but Nasheed who managed to get just 25 per cent in first round went on to defeat Gayoom in the run-off. At that time, this was made possible because everybody in the opposition had supported Nasheed, as people were tired of the longest-serving dictator and wanted a change. On this occasion, however, Yameen achieved victory by misuse of democratic institutions and blatant use of money power.

There was nothing wrong in Gasim Ibrahim going to court, but the Maldivian judiciary could not have been expected to work in an unbiased fashion given the tremendous influence Gasim enjoyed over it. He was a member of the Judicial Oversight body, Judicial Services Commission (JSC), besides being a resort tycoon and heading the Villa group of companies. He also headed the Special Majlis that drafted the 2008 Constitution and served as the Finance Minister from 2005-2008 in the Gayoom administration. During his tenure as finance minister expenditure on civil servants' salaries and allowances tripled and the government employed almost 12 per cent of the population. Moreover, in the past, when one of the Supreme Court judges, Ali Hameed, was embroiled in a controversy involving obscene conduct, Gasim Ibrahim had ensured that no action was taken against him.

Naturally, Nasheed's party, the MDP apprehended that the courts would delay the election process. It demanded reconvening of the parliament. In a statement, the party said, "We will not allow a courthouse that consists of some disgraced judges who face allegations of lewd conduct to abrogate the will of the people and disrupt the constitution."[3] The MDP was also wary of the judiciary as a similar confrontation earlier had cost Nasheed dear, as he was forced to resign as president.

The election held on September 7, 2013, was one of the most closely observed elections. It had more than 2,000 observers from various countries including India for less than 2.5 lakh voters. Besides, an NGO, Transparency Maldives, was also part of the observers' group. All the observers certified that elections were free and fair. Transparency Maldives stated that incidents taking place during the election process were not such that could have altered the election results.

International organisations like the UN and other observer countries including the US and India had urged the candidates to accept the election results and not get into litigation. But this request was not accepted by the Jumhooree Party candidate, Gasim Ibrahim.

Nonetheless, the Supreme Court of Maldives on the basis of a 'secret police report' that has not been made public yet annulled the elections held on September 7, 2013. What was worse, the court tried to give greater role to the police in the future conduct of elections rather than the Election Commission.[4] The Court also imposed several conditions to be fulfilled before the elections could be held. It asked the Election Commission to approve fingerprints of nearly 60,000 Maldivian voters. In the Maldives, this process would have taken not less than six months.

The Court also asked the Election Commission to get the voters' list endorsed by the top three candidates before proceeding with the elections.[5] However, except Nasheed, the other two candidates did not approve the list. So, even before elections were actually postponed on October 19, its ground was laid in the court verdict itself. The Supreme Court had actually given Abdulla Yameen and Gasim Ibrahim veto in holding the presidential elections. Thus, the Supreme Court directives were seen as nothing but a delaying tactic.

The hyperactive role of the police was also questionable. The police force surrounded the Election Commission office when it tried to conduct the run-off elections as scheduled on September 28. Similarly, police also forcibly thwarted the attempt of the Elections Commission of the Maldives (ECM) to conduct elections on October 19.[6] Thus, the Maldivian judiciary and police, the two major institutions who could have acted as guardian of democracy, showed their loyalty to individuals and not to the country or democracy. Misusing them, Nasheed's opponents managed to get the elections disrupted, which were held only after they felt confident of winning.

In the Maldives, during this period, the country's institutions worked at cross purposes. While the Election Commission was trying to hold elections as soon as possible, the police and judiciary were trying to delay it. Things were made worse by Waheed's attempt to cling to power. Since Waheed's term was ending on November 11, 2013, and the second round of elections were to be held on November 16, the country virtually had no government in the interregnum. The MDP proposed that Waheed should resign, and in his place, the parliament speaker should be the head of government for the interim period in order to avert a constitutional crisis. Waheed however didn't agree. Waheed was probably drawing strength not only from the opponents of Nasheed but also from some extra-regional powers who wanted to enhance their presence in the Maldives.

This attempt to manipulate institutions was also seen during the parliamentary elections that were held on March 22, 2014. Prior to these elections, judiciary once again played a hyperactive role. The Supreme Court summoned the Election Commission members on February 27, 2014 and began a surprise trial on charges of contempt of court under new 'suo-moto' regulations that allow the apex court to initiate proceedings and act as both prosecution and judge.[7] The court sacked the Election Commissioner, Fuwad Thowfeek, on March 9 and slapped him with a suspended six-month jail sentence for contempt of court. His deputy, Ahmed Fayaz, was also fired but was not given a jail sentence. Thowfeek was punished for speaking against the court's controversial role in the chaotic presidential election in 2013.

The decision to sack the Election Commission chief was criticised by the international community including India, the US, UK, EU, Commonwealth and UN.[8] The Commonwealth Secretary General said that for "a democracy to function effectively, it is critical that institutions operate within their own constitutional mandate and do not encroach either on the ability of other independent institutions to execute their own remits or on the constitutional authority of other branches of government".[9] The Maldivian Government and the courts however asked the international partners to respect the Maldivian Constitution.[10] Subsequently, the president appointed a new member, Ismail Habeeb, to the Commission, enabling the body to function with the legally required quorum.

The sacking of the chairman and deputy chairman of the Maldivian Election Commission left the election-holding body headless. It also led to the allegation that the Maldivian Supreme Court did it in an attempt to undermine the independence of the Election Commission.

The presidential elections and subsequently parliamentary elections were conducted in the Maldives without any major incident, the problem was however found in other aspects. Some people were arrested distributing cash close to the polling booths. The subversion of the Election

Commission and the use of money power created a general environment of disillusionment among the Maldivians.

A survey conducted by the anti-corruption organisation, Transparency International in 2014, pointed to a crisis of public confidence in key democratic institutions. It revealed that the parliament, parties, and the judiciary, the pillars of democracy, were the most corrupt institutions of the Maldives. Citizens appeared cynical: Politicians in their view were lying to get elected and were hardly concerned about the welfare of the ordinary people.

In this survey, 62 per cent of respondents said that they had no confidence at all in the parliament, while 58 per cent expressed lack of confidence in political parties. Nearly 50 per cent citizens expressed lack of confidence in local governments and 46 per cent in courts. Politics which included conflict, corruption, and the party system was seen as the most important problem facing the country by 77 per cent of the Maldivians.[11] Half of the people were dissatisfied with the way democracy operated in the Maldives. Political leaders enjoyed a low rating and hardly any leader was seen as better than average. Most Maldivians thought that the power was concentrated in the hands of a very small number of people. This poses a strong challenge before the democratic institutions in the Maldives to establish their credibility.

In the 2014 parliamentary polls, the Progressive Coalition of Yameen, Gasim Ibrahim and the Maldives Development Alliance (MDA) secured 53 out of 85 seats. The PPM won 33 seats, followed by the MDP with 26 seats, the Jamhooree Party with 15 seats, the MDA with five seats, independent candidates with five seats, and the Adhaalath Party with one seat (see Table 7). However, no party got the 43 seats needed to achieve a simple majority on its own. Shortly after the polls, three out of the five independent candidates as well as the MDP MP-elect, Mohamed Musthafa, signed for the ruling party, bringing the PPM's numbers to 37 MPs.

Table 7: The 2014 Maldivian parliamentary (People's Majlis) election results

#	*Political Parties*	*Seats*	*Votes Cast*	*Votes Cast (%)*
1	Progressive Party of Maldives (PPM)	33	52,960	28.2
2	Maldivian Democratic Party (MDP)	26	77,178	41.2
3	Jumhooree Party	15	24,739	13.2
4	Maldives Development Alliance (MDA)	5	7,816	4.2
5	Adhaalath Party	1	4,930	2.6
6	Dhivehi Rayyithunge Party (DRP)	0	548	0.3
7	Independents	5	19,351	10.3
		85	187,522	100
	Total Valid Votes Cast		187,522	
	Total Invalid Votes		2,120	
	Total Votes Cast		189,642	
	Total Registered Voters		240,652	
	Turnout (%)		78.8	
	National Observers	1,718		
	Media Monitors	1,924		
	Candidate Representatives	1,400		

Source: Report of the Commonwealth Observer Group, Maldives People's Majlis Election, March 22, 2014, p. 41, at http://thecommonwealth.org/sites/default/files/news-items/documents/Maldives%20People's%20Majlis%20Election %202014%20Commonwealth%20 Observer%20Group%20Report.pdf.

Breaking-up of the Progressive Alliance and Change of Political Scenario

The parliamentary elections in the Maldives gave the Progressive Coalition nearly a two-thirds majority in the parliament. For a while it appeared that the democracy in the Maldives has reached full circle as forces loyal to Gayoom were back in power and the Supreme Court was dominated by judges recruited during Gayoom era. Many announced that Gayoom had come back in style; some feared that there could be reassertion of dictatorship in the Maldives.

The nascent multi-party democracy in the Maldives had been facing pressure from three quarters – the remnants of Gayoom era, some international players who wanted to enhance their presence in the Indian Ocean, and the Islamist extremists. After losing the presidential election,

Nasheed and the MDP were hoping to get a majority in the parliament. That would have allowed them to put some check on President Yameen, as political power in the Maldives is divided between the president and the parliament. The MDP had also planned that it would use its majority in the parliament to work for reformjng the Maldivian institutions. But as the PPM got control of the parliament as well, the MDP feared that the PPM would use it to curtail civil liberties.

The MDP had more or less reconciled itself to this new situation. The party now wanted to go for internal restructuring. The position of both the president and vice president of the party was vacant after its president, Ibrahim Didi, and vice president, Alhan Fahmy, were removed in a no-confidence vote in April 2012. Nasheed now wanted new people to come forward who could run the party with greater aplomb.

This political scenario in the Maldives however changed sooner than it was expected. The 'Progressive Alliance' that was the key force behind the Yameen victory in both the presidential as well as parliamentary elections faced imminent trouble soon after. Gasim Ibrahim, the leader of the Jumhooree Party, whose support was crucial for Yameen's victory during the presidential polls, and subsequently for PPM in the parliamentary polls, wanted the post of parliament speaker. The PPM however was unwilling to give this post to him. It wanted its own candidate, Abdulla Maseeh, to become the speaker. Abdulla Maseeh eventually became the speaker by trouncing Gasim Ibrahim, but it happened at the cost of the coalition.

Gasim Ibrahim alleged that the PPM had promised to share 35 per cent of the political posts with the Jumhooree Party and to include the party in the decision-making, but it had now gone back on the promise.[12] For the deputy speaker's post, the Jumhooree Party supported the MDP candidate, Moosa Manik, who won, defeating the PPM candidate by one vote. Soon after the PPM decided to recall all political posts granted to the Jumhooree Party under the coalition agreement, and all its ministers were sacked immediately.

Blaming Gasim Ibrahim for the breakup of the alliance, Vice President Dr. Mohamed Jameel Ahmed stated that the people supported the coalition during the elections to establish a government that had no affiliation with the opposition MDP. He argued that the foundation of the PPM-

Jumhooree Party coalition was built upon achieving that goal, and that the Jumhooree Party had "turned their back" by associating with the MDP openly after the elections. He also alleged that this association indicated that the Jumhooree Party members are putting their own interests before that of people.

Islamists under Abdulla Yameen

Protection of Sunni Islam was an important issue in the run-up to the presidential elections of 2013. In his presidential campaign Yameen had presented himself as a saviour of Islam. In his election speeches he had made it clear that there should be no space for other religions in the Maldives. His election manifesto, among other things, pledged to implement death penalty under Sharia and strengthening of ties with Arab Muslim nations. He called his opponent, Mohamed Nasheed, as an enemy of the nation's Islamic unity.

Ever since the Yameen government took over power, the Ministry of Islamic Affairs has been working to fulfil these objectives. It now wants to block all religions except Islam; ensure that all laws and regulations adhere to Islamic principles; and develop and strengthen the Islamic Fiqh Academy to issue fatwas. The Ministry has signed an agreement with the Saudi Arabian Muslim Scholars Association to receive a grant of Rf 1.6 million ($ 104,166) for the "mutual goal" of developing and improving the study of Quran and religion. The Ministry of Education has introduced Arabic as a subject in schools, and now plans to have schools teach Quran as a subject up to grade VII. In January 2014, President Yameen vetoed a bill on marital rape as un-Islamic after a cleric's ruling.[13] His government subsequently started enforcing a Sharia law that enforces death penalty even on 10 year olds.[14] Police regularly hunts for atheists on social media on grounds of blasphemy.

The government of Yameen fears a threat to Sunni Islam in the Maldives from both domestic as well external sources. Domestically, it perceives threat from progressive and pro-democratic parties. Externally, they perceive threat from the Christian West. This perception is reflected in the foreign policy of Yameen where protecting the Islamic unity of the country and promoting Islamic characteristics internationally figure prominently. The Majlis in December 2013 passed a bill to amend the constitution to restrict the legislature from removing the clause that gives Islam the status of state religion. This bill was introduced in the parliament by an ally of Yameen, the MDA. Yameen has publicly cautioned Maldivians to remain vigilant of foreign influences that are trying to weaken their religious faith.[15] The Home Minister Umar Naseer has also warned Maldivians of the "ongoing psycholocial war" that aims to lead Maldivians astray from their faith in Islam and break up their ties of nationalism.[16]

The Adhaalath Party was also part of the winning coalition which brought Yameen to power, though the party had decided to support Yameen at the eleventh hour. In return, the Adhaalath Party had received the Islamic Affairs portfolio. However, the Adhaalath President, Sheikh Imran Abdulla, became critical of President Yameen after former Defence Minister, Mohamed Nazim, was arrested over charges of terrorism and treason. Nazim was also subsequently charged with importing and possessing illegal weapons. The consultative council of the Adhaalath Party alleged that after the assumption of power by President Yameen, corruption and violence had increased and justice had been abandoned. The Adhaalath Party also alleged that the government had misused public support and curtailed the basic rights guaranteed by the constitution. It further alleged that the government had undermined the independence of institutions and was now attempting to consolidate power by taking over the three branches of the state. Moreover, citing these, it withdrew its support from the government. Interestingly, the Adhaalath Party stated that it wanted to reform the system from within but couldn't succeed.

Some sections in Maldives fear that the country has now become a fertile ground for the Islamic State of Iraq and Syria (ISIS) recruitment. The opposition party, MDP, has alleged that about 30 Maldivian ISIS jihadists have returned home and are currently active in the country. Recently, Nasheed, too, alleged that the Maldives Islamic Affairs Minister, Sheikh Mohamed Shaheem Ali, may be facilitating recruitment of Maldivians by ISIS. He estimated that over 200 Maldivian men had been recruited by ISIS. Former Foreign Minister, Ahmed Naseem, has alleged that Yameen had aligned himself with extremists to bolster support for himself as he enjoys limited popular mandate and that he hoped to undermine the democratic, liberal opposition with their help.[17]

To combat the growing threat of radicalisation and extremism in the Maldives, Yameen established the National Counter Terrorism Centre (NCTC) on February 25, 2016. The NCTC has been mandated to act as the national focal point on all counter-terrorism and anti-terrorism efforts. The Centre will formulate counter-terrorism and anti-terrorism guidelines and procedures based on the analysis of international benchmarks and best practices. It will gather and analyse intelligence, from all state agencies, on terrorism activities and inform relevant state authorities. It will also seek to identify radicalised elements within the communities and run targeted rehabilitation programmes to those in need.[18]

Yameen seems to be following the policy of Gayoom days where the government tried to bolster its Islamic identity, but at the same time, it also took action against ultra-radical forces who posed a threat to the government.

Yameen's Suppression of the Opposition and Re-alignment of Political Forces

After the break-up of the Progressive Alliance, Nasheed raised the question of legitimacy of Yameen's government. Nasheed accused President Abdulla Yameen and PPM leader, Maumoon Abdul Gayoom, of attempting to control all powers of the state. Citing the breach of coalition agreement with the the Jumhooree Party, Nasheed alleged that the current administration was "based on a lie". He also suggested that the present government should be changed as it has the support of just 25 per cent of the voters.

Yameen soon realised that his political position was getting weak and his opponents were coming together. Probably, he also feared a repeat of the Sri Lankan situation where another very powerful Mahinda Rajapaksa was dislodged by the unity of opposition leaders under similar circumstances. To ward off this possibility, he decided to go after the opposition and the first to face the brunt was former president, Mohamed Nasheed. On March 13, 2015, Nasheed was found guilty of ordering the 'forcible kidnap and unlawful detention' of a Chief Judge of the Criminal Court in January 2012, and was sentenced by a three-judge bench, two of whom were state witnesses in the same case earlier.[19] His supporters believed that the charges were aimed at eliminating him as a challenger against incumbent President Yameen Abdul Gayoom in the 2018 presidential election.[20] Yameen's aim became clear on March 30, 2015 when the 85-member People's Majlis adopted 42-2 an amendment to the Maldives Prison & Parole Act, narrowing down the basic rights guaranteed for convicts. One of its provisions is to disqualify those serving a prison term from holding the membership of any political party. This change in law coming close on the heels of the questionable conviction of Nasheed, made MDP allege that it was designed to remove him from active politics.[21]

To tame another former ally and recent opponent, Gasim Ibrahim, Yameen went after his business interests. The actions taken by the government against his Villa group included terminating the lease on several islands slated for resort development. He was forced to soften his anti-government stand after being faced with near-bankruptcy due to measures that affected his business dealings.[22]

Gasim Ibrahim finally decided to mend fences with Yameen. He came out openly in favour of Yameen after an explosion took place on a speedboat carrying the president on September 28, 2015. Defending Yameen's government of which he was a former ally, Gasim Ibrahim said that it was his national duty to back the president after the explosion on the speedboat. However, he declined to comment on why his party had broken its ties with Yameen's coalition government.[23] The resort tycoon, who had failed in the last two consecutive presidential polls, also announced his intention to stand down from politics altogether, including the leadership of the Jumhooree Party, after the current parliamentary term, which would end in 2018.

Gasim Ibrahim has been suitably rewarded for his shift in loyalty. Now Civil Courts have started ruling in his favour.[24] Yameen has also started poaching Jumhooree Party MPs, two of whom, Bilehdhoo MP Ahmed Mubeen and Thinadhoo-South MP Abdulla Ahmed, joined the ruling PPM on November 25, 2015. Yameen however ruled out another falling out between the PPM and Jumhooree Party, and appreciated the Jumhooree Party and its leader, Gasim Ibrahim, backing the government in national interest.[25]

Yameen also penalised the Adhaalath Party President, Sheikh Imran Abdulla. He was sentenced by a court on February 18, 2016 to 12 years for anti-governments comments in a speech he made during a mass protest against Nasheed's arrest on May Day 2015. The government claims that Imran was charged for urging protesters "to confront police", a charge denied by his lawyers. The US and EU criticised this verdict, and Mark Toner, a spokesman for the US State Department, called the judicial process that led to the sentencing "deeply flawed". He called upon the Maldivian Government "to end politically motivated trials and to take steps to restore confidence and a commitment to democracy and human rights including freedom of expression and the rule of law and judicial independence".[26]

Some even suggest that Yameen has worked to reduce the influence of his half-brother, Gayoom. Gayoom had hoped his half-brother would be his cat's paw, but shorn of the power to dispense patronage he has lost control to Yameen. Yameen is purging, one by one, anyone who might be amenable to the old regime or likely to be a threat to him. The cases of former Defence Minister, Tholhath Ibrahim, who was sentenced to 10 years in jail over the military detention of a judge while ex-president Mohamed Nasheed was in office, and Yameen's Vice President, Ahmed Adeeb, who was impeached and charged with treason in October 2015 in connection with an explosion aboard President Abdulla Yameen's boat, exemplify this.[27]

Future of Multi-party Democracy in the Maldives

Yameen is trying to kill his political opposition. He has already managed to put Nasheed and Sheikh Imran behind bars and passed suitable amendments in law that bar them from participating in politics in the foreseeable future. It will be difficult for either the MDP or Adhaalath Party to throw up similar candidates immediately who can pose a challenge to Yameen in the 2018 elections. By using the state power Yameen has also managed to tame Gasim Ibrahim.

The International community is trying to build pressure against the dictatorial ways of Yameen. In its extraordinary meeting in London on February 26, 2016, the Commonwealth Ministerial Action Group (CMAG), called upon the Maldives to show progress in various areas, including political dialogue, to ensure inclusive, free, and fair elections in 2018. The ministers also expressed their concern regarding political space available to the opposition and detention or custody of opponents. They were also concerned about separation of powers, independence of the judiciary and, the independence and lawful functioning of democratic institutions.[28] The MDP has also suggested targeted sanctions against government officials and businessmen. Nasheed's legal team had submitted a list of such individuals.

Yameen however is also trying to garner international support. He sponsored a delegation of the All Party British-Maldives Parliamentary Group to visit the Maldives to assess the situation. The head of the group, David Amess was of the view that "Maldives unfortunately has been portrayed in a rather unfair fashion".[29]

Under international pressure Yameen has also offered dialogue with other political parties in the Maldives. But the opposition parties, the MDP and the Adhaalath Party do not want to take part in talks with the government until their leaders are released. They want the President of Maldives to establish more conducive environment ahead of the talks.[30]

Yameen is trying to tilt both the international as well as domestic situation in his favour. If Yameen succeeds in his attempt, then the framework of multi-party democracy may remain in the Maldives, but there may not be any credible political challenge to Yameen. This would also be reminiscent of the Maldives during the Gayoom era, where only one candidate stood any chance of winning elections.

NOTES

1. "Nasheed's Legal Team Files High Court Case to Defer Trial until after Elections," *Minivan News*, March 24, 2013, at http://minivannews.com/politics/nasheeds-legal-team-files-high-court-case-to-defer-trial-until-after-elections-55072 .
2. Leah Malone, "Adhaalath Party Quits President Waheed's Coalition," *Minivan News*, July 11, 2013, at http://minivannews.com/politics/adhaalath-party-quits-president-waheeds-coalition-61002; also see: Fazeena Ahmed, "President's Comment Will Affect Partnership: Adhaalath," *Haveeru Online*, July 10, 2013, at http://www.haveeru.com.mv/news/49970.
3. "Fears of Annulment Loom Large over Maldives Presidential Polls," *The Times of India*, September 17, 2013, at http://timesofindia.indiatimes.com/world/south-asia/Fears-of-annulment-loom-large-over-Maldives-presidential-polls/articleshow/22666163.cms.

4. J.J. Robinson, "Maldives Top Court Annuls September 7 Presidential Vote, Sets New Election," Reuters, October 7, 2013, at http://www.reuters.com/article/2013/10/07/us-maldives-election-court-idUSBRE9960S320131007.
5. Leah Malone, "Elections Commission Unable to Reach PPM and JP Leaders to Sign off on Electoral Register," *Minivan News*, October 18, 2013, at http://minivannews.com/politics/elections-commission-unable-to-reach-ppm-and-jp-leaders-to-sign-off-on-electoral-register-68879.
6. "Police Stop Maldives Presidential Election from Going Ahead," BBC News Asia, October 19, 2013 ,at http://www.bbc.com/news/world-asia-24591768.
7. Ahmed Naish, "EC Dismissals: Commonwealth, UK, EU, and India Join International Chorus of Concern," *Minivan News*, March 13, 2014, at http://minivannews archive.com/politics/ec-dismissals-commonwealth-uk-and-india-join-international-chorus-of-concern-79785#sthash.gMSSQUTv.dpbs (Accessed August 16, 2015).
8. "US Questions Maldives' Commitment to Democracy," *South China Morning Post*, March 11, 2014, at http://www.scmp.com/news/asia/article/1446081/us-questions-maldives-commitment-democracy (Accessed August 16, 2015).
9. Ali Naafiz, "World Powers Urge Maldives to fulfil democratic commitments," *Haveeru Online,* March 13, 2014, at http://www.haveeru.com.mv/news/53998.
10. Ahmed Naish, "EC dismissals: Government Calls on International Partners to respect Maldivian Constitution," *Minivan News*, March 13, 2014, at http://minivannews archive.com/politics/ec-dismissals-government-calls-on-international-partners-to-respect-maldivian-constitution-79780?utm_source= twitterfeed&utm_ medium = twitter#sthash.FeI3p2ji.dpbs; also see: "Maldives Rejects World's Criticism of Judiciary," *The Hindu*, March 13, 2014, at http://www.thehindu.com/news/international/south-asia/maldives-rejects-worlds-criticism-of-judiciary/article5780598.ece.
11. "A Crisis Of Confidence In Democratic Institutions," *Transparency Maldives*, May 13, 2014, at http://transparency.mv/en/news/news/a-crisis-of-confidence-in-democratic-institutions-37a749d808e46495a8da1e5352d03cae (Accessed August 16, 2015).
12. Ahmed Naish, "PPM MP Maseeh Elected Speaker, MDP MP 'Reeko' Moosa Manik Deputy Speaker," *Minivan News*, May 28, 2014, at http://minivannews.com/politics/ppm-mp-maseeh-elected-speaker-mdp-mp-reeko-moosa-manik-deputy-speaker-85899 (Accessed August 16, 2015).
13. Vishal Arora, "Maldives President Vetoes Marital Rape Bill As 'Un-Islamic'," *The Washington Post*, January 16, 2014, at http://www.washingtonpost.com/national/religion/maldives-president-vetoes-marital-rape-bill-as-un-islamic/2014/01/16/d8f50b8a-7ed3-11e3-97d3-b9925ce2c57b_story.html (Accessed August 19, 2015).
14. Euan McKirdy, "Children Could Get Death Penalty as Maldives Brings Back Executions," *CNN*, May 1, 2014, at http://edition.cnn.com/2014/05/01/world/asia/maldives-death-penalty/ (Accessed August 19, 2015).
15. Speaking on February 2, 2014 "Maldives Conversion to Islam Day"; also see: "President Yameen Sends Greetings on the Occasion of the Anniversary of Maldives' Adherence to Islam," Press Release by the President's Office, February 1, 2014 at http://www.presidencymaldives.gov.mv/?lid=11&dcid=13951 (Accessed August 16, 2015).
16. Speaking on January 2, 2014, on the Maldives National Day; also see: Mariyath Mohamed, "Religion and Nationalism Key Themes on National Day," *Minivan News*,

January 3, 2014, at http://minivannewsarchive.com/politics/religion-and-nationalism-key-themes-on-national-day-74456#sthash.4U6yfPvd.dpbs.

17. Sachin Parashar, "Maldives a Fertile Ground for ISIS, India Must Act: Former President Nasheed," *The Times of India*, February 21, 2015, at http://timesofindia. indiatimes. com/india/Maldives-a-fertile-ground-for-ISIS-India-must-act-Former-president-Nasheed/articleshow/46326832.cms (Accessed August 16, 2015).
18. Ali Naafiz, "Maldives Sets up Counter Terrorism Centre," *Haveeru Online*, February 25, 2016, at http://www.haveeru.com.mv/news/66833.
19. "Former Maldives President Mohamed Nasheed Jailed for 13 Years," *The Guardian*, March 14, 2015, at http://www.theguardian.com/world/2015/mar/14/former-maldives-president-mohamed-nasheed-jailed-for-13-years.
20. "Former Maldives President Nasheed Jailed for 13 Years", *The Hindu*, March 14, 2015, at http://www.thehindu.com/news/international/south-asia/maldives-expresident-jailed-for-13-years/article6991278.ece.
21. R.K. Radhakrishnan, "Mindless in Malé," *Frontline*, May 1, 2015, at http://www.frontline.in/world-affairs/mindless-in-Malé/article7098579.ece.
22. Muizzu Ibrahim and Ali Naafiz, "Maldives Court Annuls Termination of Resort Tycoon's Island Lease," *Haveeru Online*, December 13, 2015, at http://www.haveeru.com.mv/gasim_ibrahim/64779.
23. "Gasim Backs Pres Yameen, Seeks Support after Blast," *Haveeru Online*, October 19, 2015, at http://www.haveeru.com.mv/gasim_ibrahim/63226.
24. Muizzu Ibrahim and Ali Naafiz, "Maldives Resort Tycoon Wins More Resort Disputes," *Haveeru Online*, January 14, 2016, at http://www.haveeru.com.mv/gasim_ibrahim/65575.
25. Fazeena Ahmed and Mohamed Visham, "Maldives Pres Allays JP Fall-out Fears over Defections," *Haveeru Online*, November 25, 2015, at http://www.haveeru.com.mv/gasim_ibrahim/64247.
26. "Maldives Opposition Leader Jailed for 12 Years for Role in Protests," *Reuters*, February 18, 2016, at http://timesofindia.indiatimes.com/world/south-asia/Maldives-opposition-leader-jailed-for-12-years-for-role-in-protests/articleshow/51037256.cms.
27. Satyabrata Pal, "As India Seeks a Passage to the Maldives It Must Not Underestimate China," *The Wire*, February 19, 2016, at http://thewire.in/2016/02/19/as-india-seeks-a-passage-to-maldives-it-must-not-underestimate-china-or-the-archipelagos-problems-22058/.
28. T. Ramakrishnan, "Panel Calls for Political Dialogue in Maldives," *The Hindu*, February 26, 2016, at http://www.thehindu.com/todays-paper/tp-international/panel-calls-for-political-dialogue-in-maldives/article8282442.ece.
29. Mohamed Visham, "UK MPs Say Maldives Unfairly Portrayed, Unwise to Encourage Sanctions," *Haveeru Online*, February 18, 2016, at http://www.haveeru.com.mv/president_nasheed/66614.
30. T. Ramakrishnan, "Maldives Opposition May Boycott Talks with Govt.," *The Hindu*, February 25, 2016, at http://www.thehindu.com/todays-paper/tp-international/maldives-opposition-may-boycott-talks-with-govt/article8277579.ece.

6

Changing Regimes and Maldivian Foreign Policy

The foreign policy of a country generally does not change in a major way with a change of government, primarily because it is guided by national interests, which do not change dramatically with a regime change. However, sometimes domestic politics also influences it, as was the case with the Maldives where the foreign policy changed perceptibly when the country shifted from dictatorship to multi-party democracy. More significantly, changes also took place in the foreign policy under the three regimes that have come to power after the country's transition to democracy.

Some other drivers of the Maldivian foreign policy which have remained constant over the years are its small size, strategic location, and affiliation to Sunni Islam. The small size of the Maldives makes it vulnerable to coups. It has also been suggested that one of the most realistic and effective arrangements to keep small states secure is bilateral agreements with major powers which have enough military capabilities.[1] It also makes it imperative for the country to remain friendly with major powers like India, the US, and China, and join multilateral forums like the SAARC. The membership of SAARC also brings sovereign equality to the Maldives.[2]

The strategic location of the Maldives straddling important SLOCs and its proximity to Deigo Garcia, where the US central command base is positioned has aroused the interest of important world powers. In the past, countries like Iran, Libya, and the Soviet Union have shown interest in the military facilities available at the Gan Island. In recent times, countries like China and the US have been interested in getting a foothold in the Maldives. The external powers have occasionally aided and abetted political conspiracies bringing political instability to the country. Being a 100 per cent Sunni Muslim country, the Maldives has also been close to the Islamic world especially the Gulf countries. For the most part of its history, the Maldives has generally been independent. This love for independence is also seen in the present generation of Maldivians who want the government to follow an independent foreign policy. In the past, the Maldives has followed successfully a foreign policy which has elicited developmental support from all sides while retaining the independence of sorts in action which belies its size.[3]

Maldives and Indian Interests

Before discussing the foreign policy of the Maldives under various regimes, it is important to list out the Indian interests there. This will help us to understand the attitude of various regimes in the Maldives towards India. First, India is interested in the political stability in the neighbourhood, and the Maldives is no exception. Second, India would like to prevent the Maldives from falling under the influence of any forces (state or non-state) that are inimical to its security interests. This can also change security environment in the Indian Ocean region (IOR). Third, a large number of Indians work in the Maldives and India is interested in their safety and security. Finally, India would like the investments of its companies in the Maldives to be secure.[4]

Foreign Policy of the Maldives after Independence (Since 1965)

Immediately, after its independence from Britain, Maldives became a member of the UN in September 1965. Its objectives behind joining this World body were to end the isolation of the country. It also felt that the membership of the UN will provide the much needed security to these islands which are located in strategic but vulnerable position. Moreover, the Maldives hoped to get badly needed technical assistance. It also felt that the contact with the diplomats from all over the world would bring opportunities to develop its trade.

The Maldivian representatives attended the UN sessions intermittently till 1975. Maldives during this period in its foreign policy projected the framework of a third world country and talked of principles of non-alignment and peaceful coexistence. It also remained in favour of disarmament, nuclear non-proliferation, banning of nuclear weapons, declaration of the Indian Ocean as a Zone of Peace and independence of colonial countries. The imperatives of development induced the Maldives to become a member of several UN agencies and other inter-government organisations.

In South Asia, the Maldives has quite close relationship with Sri Lanka, India and Pakistan. Its relationship with Bangladesh has also deepened in recent times. From Sri Lanka, Maldivians bought their staple food – rice and sold fish in return. They were also getting their other ancillary foodstuff from Sri Lanka. This situation also allowed Ceylonese traders to indirectly influence Maldivian politics. Gayoom considered Sri Lanka as Maldives' gateway to the world. Initially, Maldives had its only permanent mission in Colombo which was closed in 1976 to be reopened later again in 1979. In 1981, Sri Lanka opened a permanent mission in Malé.

India was however, the first country to open a resident mission in Malé in 1976. India-Maldives relationship had started deepening since 1960s when a number of Maldivian students came to study in India under Colombo Plan. A State Bank of India branch was opened in Malé in 1974 and an airline service commenced in 1975. In 1978, the International Airport Authority of India won an international tender to expand the runway of Hulhule airport and modernize it. It completed its work in 1981. Both countries also signed an agreement to abolish visa between them. In 1980, India and the Maldives signed a trade agreement. Besides, India has also been providing technical assistance in various fields as desired by the Maldivian government. In July 1982 there was a small dispute between India and the Maldives over the Minicoy Island. However, subsequently Maldives clarified that it was not laying any political claim over Minicoy and was talking only of cultural similarity. In 1976, a Maritime Agreement was signed between the Maldives, Sri Lanka and India to demarcate their respective jurisdiction in the territorial waters on the Media Line principle.

Maldives also has significant relationship with Pakistan in South Asia. Pakistan also has its mission in Malé. In 1940s a small number of Pakistanis were employed by the British on Gan base. Pakistan has also provided technical assistance to Malé. Former president Gayoom had once sought the services of a Pakistani constitutional expert for drafting a new constitution.

Foreign Policy under Gayoom

The Maldivian foreign policy during President Maumoon Abdul Gayoom era was indifferent to India though Gayoom successfully managed to create the impression that he was friendly to India. India had saved his regime in 1988 from a coup, still he did not give any special privilege to India.[5] Most of the Indian troops were withdrawn once order was restored and only a small number of soldiers remained on the island to protect Gayoom for a year. Actually, before calling for Indian help Gayoom had requested the Western powers especially the US to come to his rescue. But they wanted India to intervene. In the later part of his regime, Gayoom tried to play China against India, as the democratic movement started to gather momentum. Gayoom probably feared that democratic India may not support him as strongly in the face of a democratic upsurge in his own country. This insecurity prompted him to look for new international partners. In this quest he started relying increasingly on China, an emerging global power with important strategic interests in the Indian Ocean.[6]

China and the Maldives established their diplomatic relationship on October 14, 1972. Since then the Chinese have been trying to build on it with various economic programmes and high-level visits. The bilateral relationship received a big boost when the Government of Maldives opened its embassy in Beijing on August 20, 2007. The Chinese managed their diplomatic relations until 2007 from their embassy in Colombo which was accredited to the Maldives.

Gayoom visited China for the first time in 1984. He went to China once again in September 2006, which further deepened the relations between Maldives and China.[7] China has tried to make inroads in countries that are of strategic importance to them by engaging in infrastructural projects. The Maldives is no exception. From 1985 the Chinese companies began entering the project-contracting business in the Maldives. By the end of 2001, the accumulated value of their contracted projects in the Maldives was $ 46.37 million, with the turnover touching $ 40 million.[8]

China has built the Maldivian Foreign Ministry building and a museum which houses the Ministry of Culture and Heritage. The Chinese have also built several housing projects in Malé apart from building the roads and drainage system in the city.[9] The Chinese have built a reputation for themselves for completing projects on time. The Chinese allocate a certain amount of funds for the Maldives every year for their activities in the country. China also provided assistance to the Maldives following the disastrous tsunami of 2004.[10]

Foreign Policy under Nasheed

Under Nasheed's term, climate change and global warming were a priority concern, though they were part of Gayoom's foreign policy, too. For his efforts to highlight the problem of climate change, Nasheed earned the epithet of Island President. As the Maldives is steadily sinking, Nasheed when in power wanted to keep some funds apart for purchasing land elsewhere. He successfully highlighted this problem on various international fora and presented climate change as a human rights issue, as it was threatening peoples' right to life. In March 2009, the Maldives declared its intention to become the first carbon-neutral country in the world within a decade. To draw the attention of the world to this problem Nasheed and his cabinet members held an underwater cabinet meeting on October 17, 2009.[11] Nasheed was the guest of honour at the Delhi High Level Conference on Climate Change and Technology Transfer,[12] and discussed with the Indian leaders the issue of climate change prior to the Copenhagen meeting.[13] Moreover, he urged for international action against global warming at the UN Summit on global warming, and pointed out that if left unattended the problem of climate change would turn from an environmental threat to a security threat.

After climate change, the most dramatic change in the Maldivian foreign policy was the establishment of diplomatic relationship with Israel.

Nasheed disclosed this when he was addressing the UN General Assembly on September 24, 2009.[14] Economic benefit was a major consideration behind this decision. He also expressed his support for an independent and sovereign Palestinian homeland. In the speech he also called for the release of Aung San Suu Kyi of Myanmar and expressed his abhorrence for terrorism in all its forms.

In the Maldives, however his decision to establish relationship with Israel came under severe criticism. The opposition party, DRP virtually declared a war against his government. This also angered his ally, the Adhaalath Party.

The Sino-Maldivian bilateral relationship however entered into a phase of uncertainty with the start of multi-party democracy in the country. Nasheed during his visit to India before the October 2008 multi-party presidential elections openly accused Gayoom of cosying up to China.[15] He promised that if his party came to power he would not be doing so. This could have been a ploy to seek Indian support and also to put pressure on Gayoom so that he would not postpone elections, as he had done in the past.

Nonetheless, even under Nasheed there was no damage to the Sino-Maldivian bilateral relationship, and if anything it continued to develop. The Maldivian government signed a Memorandum of Understanding (MoU) with the China National Machinery & Equipment & Export Corporation (CMEC) for construction of 4,000 housing units in Malé and other atolls on August 27, 2009. Maldives was required to make payment for this project over an extended period of time. The Chinese were however aware that with the coming to power of Nasheed their diplomatic influence in the Maldives had gone down. This became evident from the statements issued after high-level visits. When President Nasheed visited China on May 2, 2010 and held talks with Chinese President Hu Jintao, the latter expressed his willingness "to join hands with Maldives to strengthen political mutual trust and expand pragmatic cooperation".[16]

In early 2011, the speaker of the Maldivian Parliament, Abdulla Shahid, visited China.[17] He was greeted by Wu Bangguo, Chairman of the Standing Committee of the National People's Congress (NPC). Wu expressed China's desire to maintain friendly exchanges and cooperation at all levels in an effort to expand mutual trust and economic and trade cooperation in fields such as fisheries, tourism, and infrastructure building, so that it would be a model for relations between big and small nations. China encouraged its companies to further participate in the Maldives' national construction and encouraged more Chinese tourists to visit the country. Wu Bangguo paid a return visit to the Maldives towards the end of May 2011 and held a bilateral meeting with Abdulla Shahid, calling for closer cooperation between the two parliaments with the aim of pushing forward bilateral relations. They also planned to take the bilateral relationship to a new level on the 40th anniversary of establishing of bilateral relations in 2012.

The Chinese engaged with the Maldives shrewdly over the issue of climate change, which they knew was a priority for Nasheed. They used the Maldivian fear of global warming and climate change to their own advantage. When the US President, George Bush, rejected the Kyoto Pact on Global Warming, the Maldives had criticised the decision. China also termed the US decision "irresponsible", although it is one of the largest emitters of carbon dioxide gas. Moreover, during his visit to the Maldives, the Chinese Premier, Zhu Rongji said in Malé that China would work with the Maldives on environmental issues.

China however took a different stand on climate change during the 2009 Copenhagen Summit. Premier Wen Jiabao had a meeting with President Nasheed and leaders of other developing countries during the Copenhagen Conference on Climate Change on December 17, 2009. In this meeting, he emphasised the importance of economic development and eradication of poverty for developing countries. Acknowledging that developing countries were most severely affected by climate change, he urged developed countries to support them in terms of technology, finance, and capacity building. He denied that China was trying to promote its interests and wanted to deal with issues "within the framework of South-South cooperation".[18] China proposed voluntary action to curb emission and also showed its readiness to cooperate with other countries. The Maldivians were aware that there was little difference between Indian and Chinese stand on climate change and both these growing economies wanted poverty reduction through economic growth, and that they wanted to tackle the problem of climate change through voluntary cuts.[19] The Maldivian policymakers during this period agreed that there should be differentiated responsibility to deal with climate change, but they also thought that a legally binding treaty was necessary. They also concurred that the US and the BRICS (Brazil-Russia-India-China-South Africa) should find a way out of the deadlock.[20] They felt that India and China should use newer technology that is environment friendly.

The Chinese have also used economic diplomacy to spread their influence in a number of countries. In the case of the Maldives, though economic and technological cooperation was started in 1981 and direct trade was restored in 1982, no significant trade was conducted until 2002, and the Maldives-China trade volume totalled $ 2.977 million, of which the Maldives' imports accounted for $ 2.975 million and its exports were at $ 2,000.[21] The Sino-Maldives economic cooperation and trade volumes are thus very insignificant. Hong Kong and Singapore serve as transit ports for most of China's exports to the Maldives. China's major exports to the Maldives consist of rice and consumer goods.

In recent years, however, China has become one of the most preferred destinations for Maldivian traders. China is also becoming an emerging market for Maldivian exporters to export their marine products such as yellowfin tuna and sea cucumber.[22]

The Maldives and China signed several bilateral agreements and MoUs to boost economic and trade relations. Among them are Agreement on Economic and Technical Cooperation as well as the Agreement on Mutual Exemption of Visas and Visa Fees. An Air Services Agreement was signed between the Maldives and Hong Kong Special Administrative Region.[23] This agreement has given a boost to the tourism industry in the Maldives.

The three main industries of the Maldives are fisheries, shipping, and tourism. The fishing industry faced a problem in 1972 when Sri Lanka the largest consumer of dry "Maldive fish", stopped importing the commodity. This industry recovered later when Japan, South Korea, and Norway began to export fresh fish from the islands. The fishing industry is once again facing problems because of the shortage of fish in the Indian Ocean around the Maldives.

The Maldives is greatly dependent on its tourism industry. This industry took off in 1972, when a few uninhabited islands around Malé were converted into resorts. It has not looked back since then. However, the 2008-2010 recession, too, had its impact on the tourism industry of the Maldives.[24]

China sensed an opportunity to increase its economic influence over the Maldives by supporting its tourism industry when it was passing through difficult times, and agreements were signed to facilitate tourism.[25] China now accounts for the largest number of tourists, surpassing the UK and other European nations. The Maldives received 120,000 Chinese tourists in 2010, representing an increase of 96 per cent from the year before.[26] The subsequent years saw further increase. The Maldivian Ambassador to China in September 2010 requested Chinese to enter into infrastructure development in the tourism sector.[27] This growing Chinese market encouraged a Maldivian airline, MEGA Maldives, to start direct flights from China to Malé International Airport – the islands' main entry point for foreign tourists.

China made a conscious attempt to encourage Chinese tourists to visit the Maldives. The Maldives also benefited from its status as an "approved destination" by the Communist Party government.[28] To facilitate Chinese tourists, China also established financial institutions in the Maldives. China UnionPay (CUP) began cash withdrawal services for cardholders in 95 per cent of the ATMs in the Maldives, after entering into a partnership with the island nation's biggest bank on March 5, 2010.[29]

However, the impact of Chinese tourists on Maldivian economy remained limited. Chinese visitors do not stay for long in the Maldives and they do not spend much money. They prefer the all-inclusive options and mostly form the mid-level segment. The average cost of hotel rooms in this type of tourism is just $ 300 per night. This has generated a debate in the Maldives as to whether this would harm the image of the Maldives as a high-end tourist destination.

However, increased Chinese tourism at a time when the Maldivian tourism industry was going through recession because of the drop in the number of Western tourists created a constituency in favour of China. Chinese tourists filled the sudden void created by the recession. Many Maldivian entrepreneurs are thankful to China for that. While it is true that the Chinese tourists do not spend much money, owners of resorts and tour operators are happy as they are able to keep their businesses running.

Further, China remained interested in the Maldives despite the ushering in of multi-party democracy, with Nasheed in power,[30] primarily, because of its important strategic interests in the country. But the sense of urgency was reduced at that time because of the progress the Chinese had achieved in Sri Lanka. To increase influence over the government, Chinese delegations continued to visit the Maldives and the media was kept uninformed.[31] The bilateral relations between China and the Maldives received a major boost after China opened its embassy in Malé on November 8, 2011. It was opened two days before the Maldives hosted the 17th SAARC Summit. Previously, only India, Sri Lanka, Pakistan, and Bangladesh had an established diplomatic presence there. China became the first non-South Asian country to open an embassy in the Maldives.[32] However, what surprised everyone was the plan of Nasheed government to sign two agreements with China for supply of military hardware and for military training. However, subsequently, the Maldives gave up this plan and decided not to do anything that compromised the security environment of the Indian Ocean.[33]

Further, President Nasheed later tried to allay Indian fears. In October 2011, he stated in Perth (Australia) on the sidelines of the biennial Commonwealth Heads of Government Meeting (CHOGM) that the Maldives "will always be India's friend" and also added that he trusted "democracy far more than any other system".

The government of Nasheed claimed to follow an 'India first' foreign policy. Nasheed recently defined this policy which means, "not to have defence exercises with other countries, not to conduct our domestic policy in a way that creates fear in India, not to give a base to the Chinese, or indeed anyone to create strategic infrastructure, like deep- water ports and airports."[34] This meant that the government under him prioritised Indian interests. It also meant that the Maldives would not do anything which could jeopardise Indian security interests. He had allowed installation of radars on 26 atolls. Indian and Maldivian navies were engaged in joint exercises. The Indian navy also provided training to the MNDF. In fact, after emerging as the top contender in the first round of the 2013 presidential elections, Nasheed told a Chinese journalist that India was the most important country for him, though he was equally close to the Western powers.

Western countries liked him because he was politically groomed by the Conservative Party of Britain and had a liberal democratic orientation. Most of his advisors were also British. The Indian establishment however was uneasy with Nasheed's close contact with the UK. It was suspected that the UK was trying to persuade the Maldives to allow either the US or the UK to have naval presence in the country. Interestingly, it was also suspected that a section of Nasheed's administration particularly his defence minister was hobnobbing with the Chinese. Many see this growing distrust along with the abrasive style of Nasheed's functioning as a reason behind India's prompt recognition of the Waheed's regime.[35]

Foreign Policy under Waheed

Under the stop-gap regime of President Waheed, the foreign policy orientation of the Maldives changed yet again. Waheed was close to China. So after taking over, when his government cancelled the contract of GMR ab initio, there were reports of China's involvement; however, Waheed denied that China had nudged him into the act.[36] He and his Minister of Defence and National Security, Colonel (Retired) Mohamed Nazim, visited China. Waheed during his visit appreciated Beijing's approach to smaller countries and its policy of non-interference in their internal affairs "unlike other influential countries".[37] Both countries signed three agreements which gave Maldives US$ 500 million in assistance.[38] Few months earlier, Waheed had also stated that the Maldives now had more access to Chinese funds for developmental projects in the country. This was a clear hint to the growing closeness between the two countries.[39] When Defence Minister Mohamed Nazim visited China in December 2012 he signed a military aid agreement with the Chinese National Defence Minister, General Liang Guanglie. Nazim also assured Guanglie that the Maldives was "willing to cement relations between the two countries and their militaries".[40]

The Chinese support for Waheed became clear during the presidential elections in 2013 when he was in power. India wanted China to join the international community in pressuring Waheed's government to hold the elections in a free, fair, and inclusive manner and as scheduled. China however refused to put any pressure on Waheed, but stated that it too wanted stability in the region.[41]

Foreign Policy under Abdulla Yameen

The broad trends of foreign policy that were seen when Waheed was in power so far have continued under Abdulla Yameen, too. In the campaign for the 2013 presidential polls, Maumoon Abdul Gayoom, Yameen's half-brother and former autocrat, had argued that Malé should distance itself from the West and India and move closer to China. Similarly, Waheed during his election campaign had clearly stated that he planned to increase ties with China and improve trade and tourism.[42] Only Nasheed after the first round of elections had stated that India was the single most important country for the Maldives.[43] Yameen, however, after the elections chose to lower the political rhetoric in recognition of strategic realities and came to India as the destination of his first foreign visit after taking office.

The foreign policy of Abdulla Yameen is driven by Islam, the need to tackle financial crisis of the Maldives, and to legitimize his regime as he has come to power after a controversial election. With this objective, he has visited a number of countries that includes India, Japan, China, and Saudi Arabia. However, the choices made by him to deal with the financial crisis are rather interesting.

After India, another major country to be visited by Yameen was Japan. His April 2014 state visit was the first official visit of a Maldivian President to Japan and was seen as an economic offensive of Yameen.[44] Japan has emerged as the biggest donor for the Maldives after their diplomatic relationship was established nearly 40 years ago in 1967. The Maldives has reciprocated by publicly announcing its full support for Japan's bid to become a permanent member of the UN Security Council.[45] A Maldivian embassy has been in Japan since 2007, but Japan only recently opened its embassy in the Maldives on February 8, 2016.[46]

During this visit Yameen held meetings with prominent businessmen, economists, and industrialists and discussed means of obtaining funds for various development projects in the Maldives.[47] Both countries showed interest in enhancing cooperation in the area of maritime security. Japan wanted the Maldives to ensure the safety of sea lanes passing nearby it.[48]

The visit of Yameen to Japan was important as the Maldives is also closely engaged with China. It is a bold strategic move for the Maldives to engage with China in order to balance India, and benefit from it economically, and at the same time, to bring in Japan and seek to balance China as well.

As expected, the Maldivian relationship with China is deepening under Yameen. Chinese companies have showed interest in major Maldivian infrastructural and communication projects that are on offer, namely in constructing a bridge between Malé and the island of Hulhule using their own funds and maintaining it for a prolonged period.[49] The Chinese completed the survey on the Malé-Hulhule Bridge Project and its cost of about $ 3-4 million was borne by the Chinese Government. The construction of the bridge is being financed through soft loan by the Chinese Exim Bank.

The Chinese embassy in the Maldives opened a visa section on January 10, 2014 in order to allow Maldivians to get Chinese visa directly from Malé. Now Maldivians can get free Chinese visa in four working days. The Chinese have given ¥ 50 million (US$ 8.2 million) in development aid to the Maldives and want to construct 1,500 housing units. The Chinese ambassador to the Maldives, Wang Fukang, also announced that both sides were working together to make the best use of Chinese grant aid and the concessional loans to further benefit the economic and social development of Maldives.[50]

China is also trying to engage the Maldives in the agricultural sector. It has signed an agreement on agricultural and research project cooperation in April 2014 to provide grant to the Maldivian farmers. Under this agreement, the Government of China would extend to the Government of Maldives a grant aid of ¥ 1 million (about US$ 160,000) which would be utilised for developing the agriculture sector.

The Chinese-Maldivian relationship took a great leap forward when Chinese President, Xi Jinping, visited the archipelago nation in September 2014. This was the first visit of any Chinese President to the Maldives since the former British protectorate gained independence in 1965. Yameen too had visited the Chinese city of Nanjing just a month earlier. Thus, the two leaders were meeting for second time within a month. This was a clear indication of the importance both sides were attaching to each other.

The most important objective of the Xi Jinping's visit to the Maldives was to get Maldivian support for his modern maritime "Silk Road". Maldives agreed to participate actively in the initiative to create a shipping route from China to Europe via West Africa.[51] Besides this, both sides signed nine agreements related to the expansion of the Maldives' main international airport, a power station project, road construction, and a bridge to connect the capital island of Malé with nearby Hulhule. The value of the projects was not made public. Maldives was also offered help to fight the threat emerging from the phenomenon of the climate change. Interestingly, China is the world's leading polluting country after the United States.

President Xi emphasised the excellent relationship that existed between the two countries and stated that China respected the independence, sovereignty, and territorial integrity of the Maldives, and the Maldivian people's choice of political system and development path according to their own national conditions. Xi expressed his desire to deepen bilateral relationship with the Maldives and build a future-oriented comprehensive friendly and cooperative partnership between the two countries.

Keeping in view the critical importance of tourism in the Maldivian economy, President Xi Jinping reassured the country that China would continue to encourage its citizens to travel to the Maldives and Chinese enterprises to invest in the Maldives' tourism industry. The Maldives on its part promised to improve its facilities in the tourism sector to better cater to the requirements of the Chinese. It also pledged to ensure the safety of Chinese tourists in the Maldives. Both sides also agreed to establish a joint meeting mechanism to deal with the issue of safety of Chinese tourists in the Maldives. It was believed that both sides did not take up sensitive security issues as it would have raised concerns in India.

Before Yameen's visit to China, then Vice President Dr Mohamed Jameel Ahmed had also gone there on an official visit in June 2014. In China, he attended the ninth China-South Asia Business Forum and the second China-South Asia Expo. In both the events he emphasised the need for foreign investment to accelerate the growth of Maldivian economy, private sector development, and wealth creation.[52]

The Maldives also obliged China by endorsing its Maritime Silk Route project in December 2014. It also decided to back a Chinese-initiated international finance institution to be called the Asian Infrastructure Investment Bank (AIIB).[53] The country expressed its desire to be included as one of the founding members of the proposed bank along with the existing 21 countries, which includes both China and India. The Maldives has already held two rounds of talks on free trade pact with China and hopes to sign the agreement either by end of 2016 or in the beginning of 2017.[54]

After China showed its interest in the Maldivian communication satellite project, the Government of India reportedly wanted to "push" the Indian Space Research Organisation (ISRO) to submit a proposal for the joint manufacturing, launch, and operations of a Maldives' communications satellite as a means to improve bilateral relations.[55] The ISRO however found the project not viable and was willing to participate only if the Indian Ministry of External Affairs agreed to partly subsidise the project. The Maldives however denied receiving any proposal from India.[56]

The growing economic and military power of China along with its dependence on energy sources coming from the Gulf and Africa has made Chinese interested in the Maldives. China has also figured prominently in the foreign policy of every Maldivian Government. Both Gayoom and his successor, Mohamed Nasheed, had courted China over the last few years. They had received billions of dollars in investment in the Maldives which reduced dependence of the country on India. Waheed was openly pro-China. But as far as Abdulla Yameen is concerned, his love for China to balance India remains, but is more guarded in his approach now.

Further, Yameen is also trying to take Maldives closer to Saudi Arabia. Though both countries had established their diplomatic relationship in 1981, the Maldives opened its embassy in Saudi Arabia only in 2008. It was its first ever diplomatic mission in West Asia. Saudi Arabia opened its embassy in the Maldives in August 2015.[57] The Maldives is a Sunni Muslim country like the Saudi Arabia and considers Saudi Arabia as the fountainhead of Islamic practices. There has been a tendency in the Maldives to ape the Arab culture. It was vividly seen when the country replaced its original Dives Akuru script of Dhivehi language by Thaana around 18th century, which is largely modelled on the Arabic style of writing. It is feared that the Maldives might try to replicate Saudi education system, which is extensively based on Wahabi ideology. A part of Saudi funding is also directed towards that.

Yameen during his election campaign had portrayed Nasheed as the enemy of Islamic unity in the country. His election manifesto talked of closer relationship with Arab Muslim countries among other things. Even Gayoom who had opposed radical versions of Islam and Saudi influence in religion during his rule changed his policy after getting defeated by Nasheed to expand his coalition by roping in conservative Islamic parties and organisations.[58]

The common religious ideology is not the only attraction for the Maldivians to look towards the Saudis. The acute financial crisis in the Maldives has also made the country look towards them for help. Saudis have already promised the Maldives a five-year soft loan facility of $ 300 m, pledged in July 2013 when the country's previous president, Waheed, had visited Riyadh.[59]

Yameen invited the Crown Prince of Saudi Arabia, Salman bin Abdulaziz al-Saud, who is also the Defence Minister of Saudi Arabia, on an official business visit In March 2014.[60] He helped the Maldivian economy by booking out three whole islands for nearly a month. The Maldives and Saudi Arabia decided to open air links and planned 14 flights a week. The Saudi property company, Best Choice is building a family holiday resort with world-class facilities worth $ 100 m. The Maldives is also seeking Saudi partnerships in energy and transport.

Presently, Maldives' relations with Saudi Arabia are at an all-time high as the Maldives looks to secure funding for several mega development projects of the government. Saudi Arabia has agreed to loan US$ 80 million to the Maldives for the development of the second phase of Hulhumalé, the reclaimed suburb of capital Malé. This loan was arranged "in record" time. Saudis have also agreed to provide oil to the Maldives at a discounted price. In the latter half of 2015, Saudi Arabia had also announced its decision to build new schools in the Maldives, and requested submission of relevant plans at the earliest. To reciprocate the gesture of Saudis, the Maldives has now signed up to be a part of an Islamic military alliance spearheaded by the Islamic kingdom.[61]

Fisheries where nearly 20 per cent of the workforce is employed is one of the most important industries in the Maldives. This industry however is facing pressure after the EU refused to grant duty exemption to Maldives' fish exports to Europe.[62] The Maldives has criticised this EU policy and is planning to export fish to Saudi Arabia after certifying them as halal.[63]

However, the biggest gain in cooperation between the Saudi Arabia and the Maldives is in the area of Islamic affairs. The Saudi Prince has pledged to build 10 "world-class" mosques in the archipelago. Moreover, Saudi Arabia is building the largest mosque in the island nation. The work on the King Salman Mosque has started which will accommodate more than 6,000 people at once. At the inaugural ceremony, Islamic Affairs Minister, Ahmed Ziyad said the mosque was a symbol of the priority given by the government to promote Islam.[64]

In addition, visiting Saudi scholars have pledged a grant of $ 100,000 for Islamic education. They also announced 50 scholarships for students to study in Saudi Arabia. Saudi Arabia has also donated more than 100,000 books in the Arabic language to Maldivian students. These books were sent to 60 schools across the Maldives that teach Arabic language and to another three that follow the Arabic medium.[65]

The funding from Saudi Arabia is also convenient as the country does not raise uncomfortable questions involving human rights or rising Islamic conservatism. Moreover, the funding received from them is useful in sustaining a large civil service. The Western powers who were quite active during Nasheed's time now appear apprehensive at the growing Saudi influence in the Maldives.[66]

The action of the Maldivian Government to implicate Nasheed and imprison him for 13 years was criticised the world over. Yameen's attempt to undermine the spirit of democracy disillusioned even the Jumhooree Party and the ultra-hardline, Adaalath Party who called for the formation of a 'national unity alliance' against the government. Yameen has however received support from the Chinese and Saudis. Immediately after the imprisonment of Nasheed[67] on March 14, 2015, President Yameen went to Saudi Arabia on an official visit on March 18, 2015.[68] Saudi Arabia, too, is concerned after the emergence of the Arab Spring, which has economic and democratic reforms as two important components. It senses the same tendencies even in Maldives. Hence, it is not averse to strengthen the hands of Yameen by assuring investment and trade. It is hardly surprising that both sides emphasised on "rejecting any foreign interference in their internal affairs".

Moreover, during Yameen's visit, both sides "expressed their desire to strengthen cooperation in foreign affairs, defence, Islamic affairs, justice, economic, investment and trade sectors as well as education, health and social affairs to realise their common interests".[69] They also agreed to expand trade and investment cooperation. It was decided that the Saudi Fund for Development will continue to finance development projects in the Maldives including expansion of Malé International Airport and protection of the country's coastal areas. To deepen educational and cultural cooperation, Saudi Arabia agreed to provide 150 scholarships to Maldives' students. President Yameen declared that the Maldives considered Saudi Arabia its first political and business partner.[70]

The Maldivian Government has been trying to expand the Malé airport. During Yameen's visit, Saudi Arabia assured loan assistance at a low interest rate of two per cent from the Saudi Fund to finance this project.

In recent times, Saudis have also wanted to reduce their dependence on the US. With this objective, they have been following a 'look east policy' since the middle of the last decade. They have used their 'custodian of holy mosque' card with the non-oil Islamic countries like the Maldives to ensure a patron-client relationship based on 'Islamic unity'. Saudis also think that having a friendly relationship with the Maldives would protect their long-term interests, as Maldives is located at a crucial point from where their large chunk of oil supply passes through.

Interestingly, the impact of Saudi education is not uniform and does not necessarily result in support for the Kingdom's government. It also produces radical Wahabis who are highly critical of the country's ruling elite. Still, Saudis follow the Wahabi School of Philosophy in their education model and fund such education worldwide. In 2005, Saudis had decided to allocate US$ 35 billion for building mosques in South Asia. Besides, a large number of madrassas have also come up. Saudis are known to fund such madrassas which promote anti-Shia Islam and allow the rise of fanatical Taliban-type fighters. They have done it in Pakistan, and they can do it in the Maldives, too. There have been reports in the past which indicated that the Taliban has recruited hundreds of Maldivians who are fighting in Pakistan.

In recent times, ISIS seems to have caught the fancy of the Maldivian youth. During Yameen's visit to Saudi Arabia, both sides talked of fighting extremism and terrorism in all their forms and manifestations, as they believe their countries are based on "tolerant principles of Islam", hinting at a joint cooperation to check the menace of ISIS. Saudi Arabia is no longer enamoured with the ISIS, as its leaders want to promote pristine Wahabi ideology which poses existential threat to the Kingdom's monarchy.

The MDP believes that about 200 Maldivians have been recruited by the ISIS. A jihadi group called Bilad Al Sham Media (BASM) describes itself as 'Maldivians in Syria', and claims that five Maldivians have already died in Syria. If both Saudi Arabia and the Maldives decide to jointly fight ISIS, then it would be a welcome move and could actually improve the security scenario in the IOR. However, if these countries chose to follow Pakistan model, then it would worsen it. It is possible that Saudi Arabia can use its financial resources to support Al Qaeda and Lashkar-e-Taiba to foil the rise of ISIS. The ordinary Maldivian may not like his country to become a fertile ground for extremism and terrorism as he has sacrificed a lot to get democracy.

Though the relationship of the Maldives with Pakistan goes back to the 1940s when a small number of Pakistanis were employed by the British on the Gan base, Maldivians have been taking a measured stand on issues like Kashmir. Gayoom even stated that he does not look at the Kashmir issue through religious lens and wanted both India and Pakistan to sort it out bilaterally.[71] However, in recent times, there has been a change in bilateral relationship mostly because of people-to-people contact after a number of Maldivians started going there to study in various madarssas.

The Maldives is also trying to intensify military-to-military relationship with Pakistan. The Maldivian Chief of Defence Force, Maj. Gen. Ahmed Shiyam visited Pakistan in March 2014. During his visit the Maldives and Pakistan discussed expansion in defence relations in military training, joint military exercises, and defence production.[72]

Implications for India

The Maldives has seen only two multi-party elections; however, it has seen three governments by three political parties which are different from one another in their political orientation. It is only to be expected that they would follow different foreign policies.

Nasheed is a liberal democrat and during his short stint followed an India friendly policy. India and the Maldives had close defence and economic engagement. Commercial interests of Indian companies were protected and promoted in the Maldives. All this however changed the moment Waheed came to power.

The Waheed government started on a clearly anti-India note – terminating the GMR contract ab-initio. The decision was not just a result of domestic politics, but also under external influence, especially of China. Under Waheed, India's influence over the Maldives reached its nadir. India wanted a smooth political transition in the Maldives through free and fair elections. Moreover, the Indian Foreign Secretary, Sujatha Singh, had visited the Maldives to persuade Maldivian authorities to hold the run-off presidential election. Despite India's efforts, the opponents of Nasheed managed to get the elections scuttled.

At the same time, there was a significant increase in China's influence, which already has a firm presence in Sri Lanka. During Waheed's period, the Maldives as chair of the SAARC was also working to bring China into the regional organisation.

Waheed adopted an unusual confrontational attitude with regard to India. He resented India's role as facilitator in the Maldivian presidential elections and stated that foreign powers should stay out of Maldives. The Maldivian Foreign Ministry even called the Indian Ambassador, Rajeev Sahare, to raise the issue of his meeting with the Maldivian Election

Commission. The actions of the Waheed government raised the important question about the source of his strength.

India had erred in the judgment of Waheed's regime. It was too quick in offering recognition to that regime. The official Indian response to the transfer of power in 2012 was based on feedback from the Indian High Commission in Malé which certified Waheed as pro-India.[73] Subsequently, however, when India went for course correction, it identified itself too closely with Nasheed's regime. That also proved to be a hindrance once Nasheed lost the elections.[74]

After deteriorating considerably under Abdulla Yameen in the beginning, now there is a thaw in the India – Maldives bilateral relationship. Though an attempt was made to patch the gulf between him and India,[75] the bonhomie of Nasheed days has not returned. Yameen made clear that though he wanted to improve the relationship with India, but that did not mean that the contract of GMR would be renewed. On the other hand, he asked his government to make arrangement for the payment to GMR, as Maldives had lost the arbitration case in Singapore.

The unceremonious exit of GMR from the Maldives highlights that India will have to take a closer view on Indian investments abroad. So far the Indian Government has taken a stand that it has nothing to do with a commercial agreement between two entities. Of course, the government can choose to go by local laws in cases of business dispute, but if India wants to project the image of a confident regional power, then it will have to do more.

In the political crisis that emerged after Nasheed's removal, India could not steer events in the Maldives. Its foreign policy towards the Maldives appeared confused. India appeared to be following the US line on the Maldives and Sri Lanka on issues of its concern. Often it merely reacted to situations. It appeared as if India was having no long-term view on where India-Maldives relations should be heading.[76] While Indians were denouncing Waheed for suppressing democracy, Americans were trying to negotiate SOFA with his government. However, this effort of Americans got exposed and the deal could not materialise.[77] The India-Maldives bilateral relationship seems to be somewhat improving after the visit of Indian foreign minister Sushma Swaraj in October 2015 when India tried to mend fences. The repeated misreading of the situation in the Maldives since late 2011 has caused problems in India-Maldives bilateral relations. Reversing this is going to take concerted effort and time.

NOTES

1. Hideyuki Takahashi, "Maldivian National Security – And the Threats of Mercenaries," *The Round Table*, 88 (351), 1999, p. 437.
2. Amrita Banerjee, "Maldives & SAARC," *World Focus*, March 2012, p. 54.
3. Urmila Phadnis and Ela Dutt Luithui, "The Maldives Enter World Politics," *Asian Affairs*, 8. (3), January-February 1981, p. 175.
4. N Manoharan, "An Agenda for the New Government: Policy Options for India in Maldives," Issue Brief # 248, March 2014, at http://www.ipcs.org/pdf_file/issue/IB250-Manoharan-Maldives.pdf (Accessed August 17, 2015).
5. "India Sends Troops to Maldives to Crush Coup Attempt by Invading Mercenaries," *Los Angeles Times*, November 04, 1988, at http://articles.latimes.com/1988-11-04/news/mn-961_1_coup-attempt (Accessed August 14, 2014); also see: Sanjoy Hazarika, "Indian Troops End Coup In Maldives," *The New York Times*, November 5, 1988, at http://www.nytimes.com/1988/11/05/world/indian-troops-end-coup-in-maldives.html (Accessed August 16, 2015).
6. "China Is Most Reliable Friend: Maldivian President," *Xinhua*, April 17, 2006, at http://english.people.com.cn/200604/17/eng20060417_258847.html (Accessed August 16, 2015).
7. "China, Maldives Enhance Ties," *CCTV.com*, September 13, 2006, at http://www.cctv.com/english/20060913/100488.shtml (Accessed August 16, 2015).
8. "China and Maldives," Ministry of Foreign Affairs, People's Republic of China, October 23, 2003, at http://www.mfa.gov.cn/eng/wjb/zzjg/yzs/gjlb/2737/t16076.htm (Accessed August 16, 2015).
9. Gathered from the author's field visit.
10. "Maldivian President Meets with Chinese Delegation," *Xinhua*, January 11, 2005, at http://english.people.com.cn/200501/11/eng20050111_170215.html (Accessed August 16, 2015).
11. "Maldives Government Dives for Climate Change," *The Hindu*, October 17, 2009, at http://beta.thehindu.com/news/international/article35268.ece?css=print (Accessed August 16, 2015).
12. B. Muralidhar Reddy, "Maldivian President on Five-Day Visit to India," *The Hindu*, October 20, 2009, at http://beta.thehindu.com/news/article36073.ece (Accessed August 16, 2015).
13. B. Muralidhar Reddy, "Climate Change, Bilateral Ties Top Nasheed's Agenda for India Visit," *The Hindu*, October 19, 2009, at http://beta.thehindu.com/news/international/article35734.ece?css=print (Accessed August 16, 2015).
14. "Maldives to the General Debate of the General Assembly," New York, 24 September 2009,
15. "Maldives Opposition Leader Warns of Rising Chinese Influence," Thaindian.com, July 10, 2008, at http://www.thaindian.com/newsportal/uncategorized/maldives-

opposition-leader-warns-of-rising-chinese-influence_10070188.html; also see: "Maldives's China Policy a Security Threat to India," Thaindian.com, July 10, 2008, at http://www.thaindian.com/newsportal/india-news/maldivess-china-policy-a-security-threat-to-india_10070110.html (Accessed July 15, 2008).

16. "Hu Jintao Holds Talks with President of Maldives Nasheed," Ministry of Foreign Affairs, People's Republic of China, May 2, 2010, at http://www.fmprc.gov.cn/eng/zxxx/t689890.htm (Accessed August 16, 2015).
17. Zheng Jie and Che Hongliang, "Maldives-China Ties to Continue to Prosper: Maldivian Parliament Speaker," *Xinhua*, May 28, 2011, at http://english.people.com.cn/90001/90776/90883/7393725.html (Accessed August 16, 2015).
18. "Wen Jiabao Meets with Maldivian, Ethiopian, Bangladeshi, Grenadian, Sudanese Leaders," Ministry of Foreign Affairs, People's Republic of China, December 18, 2009, at http://www.mfa.gov.cn/eng/wjb/zzjg/yzs/gjlb/2737/2739/t646720.htm.
19. A top policymaker in Ministry of Housing and Environment, in an interview to the author.
20. Another top policymaker in an interview to author.
21. "Maldives-China Relations," Embassy of Maldives in China, at http://www.maldivesembassy.cn/Maldives&china.asp (Accessed August 16, 2015).
22. Ibid.
23. Ibid.
24. From interviews conducted during the author's field visit.
25. "China to Encourage Its Tourists to Visit Maldives," *Miadhu Daily*, May 3, 2010, at http://www.miadhu.com/2010/05/local-news/china-to-encourage-its-tourists-to-visit-maldives/ (Accessed May 15, 2010).
26. "China Becomes Maldives' Largest Source of Tourists," *People's Daily Online*, May 12, 2011, at http://english.peopledaily.com.cn/90001/90776/90882/7378362.html (Accessed May 15, 2011).
27. Wang Zhaokun, "Maldives Woos Chinese Investors," *Global Times*, September 26, 2010, at http://world.globaltimes.cn/asia-pacific/2010-09/577067.html (Accessed October 10, 2010).
28. "Maldives Now a Destination of Choice for Chinese Visitors," *The South China Morning Post*, September 23, 2013, at http://www.scmp.com/news/china/article/1315895/chinas-tourists-diplomats-make-splash-maldives (Accessed October 10, 2013).
29. B. Raman, "China In Maldives," Paper No. 3704, South Asia Analysis Group, March 08, 2010, at http://www.southasiaanalysis.org/%5Cpapers38%5Cpaper3704.html (Accessed August 10, 2015).
30. "China Vows to Expand Military Cooperation with Maldives," *Xinhua*, February 19, 2009, at http://news.xinhuanet.com/english/2009-02/19/content_10851296.htm (Accessed March 10, 2010).
31. Adam Lateef, editor, *Miadhu Daily*, during an interview with the author.
32. Priyabhishek Sharma, "China Factor in Indo-Maldivian Relations," *World Focus*, September 2014, p. 31.
33. Based on interview conducted during the author's field visit in the Maldives.

34. Interview of Nasheed in the Hindu by Parvathi Menon, "'Maldives is sitting on a time bomb'," The Hindu, March 4, 2016 at http://www.thehindu.com/opinion/interview/interview-with-nasheed-mohamed/article8310022.ece
35. S.D. Muni, "Stabilising the Neighbourhood?: India's Flip Flop Approach to Maldives Crisis," ISAS Working Paper No. 145, March 16, 2012, p. 10.
36. R. K. Radhakrishnan, "Maldives Denies China Role in GMR Row," *The Hindu*, December 10, 2012, at http://www.thehindu.com/news/international/maldives-denies-china-role-in-gmr-row/article4181805.ece.
37. "Maldivian President Lauds China's 'Non-interference'," *The Hindu Business Line*, September 2, 2012, at http://www.thehindubusinessline.com/news/international/maldivian-president-lauds-chinas-noninterference/article3851013.ece; also see, "News Analysis: Maldives President Lauds China's Foreign Policy," *Xinhua*, September 01, 2012, at http://english.peopledaily.com.cn/90883/7932522.html.
38. Ahmed Hamdhoon, "Maldives Signs Agreements Worth USD500 Million with China," *Haveeru Online*, September 03, 2012, at http://www.haveeru.com.mv/news/44329.
39. "Have More Access to Chinese Funds, Says Maldives President Mohamed Waheed," *The Economic Times*, July 9, 2013, at http://articles.economictimes.indiatimes.com/2013-07-09/news/40469196_1_maldives-government-maldivian-president-moh amed-waheed-only-operational-international-airport.
40. Ahmed Naish, "Defence Minister Signs Military Aid Agreement with China," *Minivan News*, December 16, 2012, at http://minivannews.com/politics/defence-minister-signs-military-aid-agreement-with-china-49018.
41. J J Robinson, "China Calls for Maldives to 'maintain national stability and social development'," *Minivan News*, October 22, 2013, at http://minivannews.com/politics/china-calls-for-maldives-to-maintain-national-stability-and-social-development-69580.
42. "Maldives President Says Intent on Boosting Ties with China," *Global Times*, *Xinhua*, September 7, 2013, at http://www.globaltimes.cn/content/809284.shtml.
43. "India Single Most Important Country for Maldives: Nasheed," *The Times of India*, September 8, 2013, at http://timesofindia.indiatimes.com/world/south-asia/India-single-most-important-country-for-Maldives-Nasheed/articleshow/22416942.cms.
44. "Visit to Japan of H.E. Mr. Yameen, President of the Republic of Maldives," Ministry of Foreign Affairs of Japan, April 8, 2014, at http://www.mofa.go.jp/press/release/press22e_000006.html.
45. "Maldives-Japan Relations", at http://www.maldivesembassy.jp/maldives-japan-relations.
46. Ali Naafiz, "Japan Opens First Embassy in Maldives," *Haveeru Online*, February 08, 2016, at http://www.haveeru.com.mv/news/66281.
47. Mariyath Mohamed, "President Yameen on Economic Offensive in Japan," April 17, 2014, at http://minivannews.com/politics/president-yameen-on-economic-offensive-in-japan-82896.
48. "Maldives, Japan to Enhance Security, Economic Ties," *Haveeru Online*, April 17, 2014, at http://www.haveeru.com.mv/news/54474.
49. "Chinese Companies among Those Interested in Maldives Mega Bridge Project," *The Global Times*, *Xinhua*, December 20, 2013, at http://www.globaltimes.cn/content/833289.shtml.

50. Daniel Bosley, Ahmed Naish, "Chinese Ambassador Announces Plans to Build 1,500 Houses in Maldives," *Minivan News,* January 29, 2014, at http://minivannews.com/news-in-brief/maldives-police-to-take-part-in-chinese-seminar-82139.
51. Christina Larson, "China's Xi Jinping Calls for Building a 'Maritime Silk Road'," Bloomberg, September 17, 2014, at http://www.bloomberg.com/bw/articles/2014-09-17/china-seeks-friends-on-the-maritime-silk-road (Accessed August 17, 2015)
52. Mariyath Mohamed, "Vice President Continues Search for Investors during China Visit," *Minivan News*, June 8, 2014, at http://minivannews.com/politics/vice-president-continues-search-for-investors-during-china-visit-86593.
53. Ismail Humaam Hamid, "Maldives Backs New Chinese Investment Bank, Pursues Free Trade Deal," *Minivan News*, December 22, 2014, at http://minivannews.com/politics/maldives-backs-new-chinese-investment-bank-pursues-free-trade-deal-91768.
54. Fathmath Shaahunaz, "Maldives, China end second free-trade talks," Haveeru Online, Mar 05, 2016 at http://www.haveeru.com.mv/business/67077
55. Leah Malone, "Maldives' Satellite Bid, Chinese Involvement Leads to India's Alleged Security Concerns," *Minivan News*, April 6, 2013, at http://minivannews.com/politics/maldives-satellite-bid-chinese-involvement-leads-to-indias-alleged-security-concerns-55790.
56. Abdullah Jameel, "Maldives Denies India Offer to Operate Satellite," *Haveeru Online*, April 6, 2013, at http://www.haveeru.com.mv/news/48314.
57. Mohamed Visham, "Saudi Arabia Opens Embassy in Maldives," *Haveeru Online*, August 3, 2015, at http://www.haveeru.com.mv/news/61346 (Accessed August 19, 2015).
58. Vishal Arora, "Maldives: A Return to Religious Conservatism," *The Diplomat*, February 17, 2014, at http://thediplomat.com/2014/02/maldives-a-return-to-religious-conservatism/.
59. Ali Naafiz, "Maldives Seeks $300 Mln Credit Facility from Saudi Arabia," *Haveeru Online*, July 16, 2013, at http://www.haveeru.com.mv/maldivessaudi/50086.
60. Farah Ahmed, "Saudi Crown Prince Arrives in Maldives," *Haveeru Online*, February 28, 2014, at http://www.haveeru.com.mv/news/53829.
61. Ali Naafiz, "Maldives Kicks off Saudi-funded Project to Build Largest Mosque," *Haveeru Online*, February 25, 2016, at http://www.haveeru.com.mv/news/66809.
62. Ahmed Naif, "Maldives to Lose Duty Free Access to EU over Lack of Religious Freedom," *Haveeru Online*, November 07, 2013, at http://www.haveeru.com.mv/news/52230.
63. Mohamed Afrah, "Maldives to Halal Certify Tuna Products," *Haveeru Online*, December 10, 2013, at http://www.haveeru.com.mv/news/52782.
64. Ali Naafiz, No. 59.
65. Asima Nizar and Ali Naafiz, "Saudi Arabia Donates over 100k Books to Maldives," *Haveeru Online*, February 24, 2016, at http://www.haveeru.com.mv/news/66789.
66. Charles Haviland, "Saudi Arabia's Growing Role in the Maldives," BBC News, March 24, 2014, at http://www.bbc.com/news/business-26668107?print=true.
67. Jason Burke, Zaheena Rasheed, "Former Maldives president Mohamed Nasheed jailed for 13 years," The Guardian, March 14, 2015 at http://www.theguardian.com/world/2015/mar/14/former-maldives-president-mohamed-nasheed-jailed-for-13-years

68. President Yameen and First Lady arrive in Saudi Arabia, The Presidency, Republic of Maldives, 18 March 2015, at http://www.presidencymaldives.gov.mv/?lid=11&dcid=15387
69. Joint Statement issued at the conclusion of Yameen's visit to the Kingdom.
70. "Kingdom Agrees to Open Embassy in Maldives," at http://www.arabnews.com/news/720731.
71. "Maldives in the 1990s," *Spotlight on Regional Affairs,* XI (3), Institute of Regional Studies, Islamabad, pp. 12-13.
72. "Maldives Defence Forces Chief Visits POF," *The Dawn*, March 12, 2014, at http://www.dawn.com/news/1092596.
73. Debanjana Chakravarti, "Evolution of the Indo-Maldivian Bilateral Relations," *World Focus*, July 2013, p. 112.
74. S.D. Muni, "The Old Order Strikes Back in the Maldives," *Tehelka*, 10 (48), November 30, 2013, at http://www.tehelka.com/maldives-the-empire-strikes-back/.
75. Mohamed Visham, "US, India Congratulate Maldives' President Elect," *Haveeru Online*, November 17, 2013, at http://www.haveeru.com.mv/news/52406.
76. R.K. Radhakrishnan, "The Maldives Angle," *Frontline*, May 28, 2014, at http://www.frontline.in/cover-story/the-maldives-angle/article6052928.ece.
77. J J Robinson, "Leaked Draft Agreement Opens Possibility for US Base in Maldives," *Minivan News*, April 24, 2013, at http://minivannews.com/politics/leaked-draft-agreement-opens-possibility-for-us-base-in-maldives-56913; also see: "A US Military Base in the Maldives?," April 24, 2013, at http://www.dhivehisitee.com/executive/us-military-base-maldives/.

7

Strategic Importance of the Indian Ocean and the Maldives

The Indian Ocean is the third-largest ocean of the world and its strategic importance lies in the fact that it truly connects the world – Europe and the Americas with West Asia, Africa, and East Asia; the island continent, Australia, is also on its rim. Moreover, it has access to four critical waterways – the Suez Canal, Bab-el Mandeb, Strait of Hormuz, and Strait of Malacca. The Republic of Maldives is a string of small coral islands situated in the middle of this ocean.

The great powers have always struggled to control the Indian Ocean because of its crucial geographical location. In the 19th century, Britain was the dominant power in the IOR and the Indian Ocean was seen as a British lake. The British dominated this region and the Indian Ocean connected India and the Far-East to London. During the World War II the entry of Japan into the Indian Ocean demonstrated clearly the entire dependence of the security of India on the mastery of the seas. The Japanese not only captured the Andaman and Nicobar Islands but also shelled the port of Visakhapatnam. However, with the start of the decolonisation process in the 20th century Britain lost its pre-eminence. Subsequently, during the Cold War period, the two superpowers, the US and the former Soviet Union struggled for dominance in these waters. In this rivalry, the

US was able to prevail and has maintained its status for the last many years. The role of the Maldives because of its important geo-strategic location in the Indian Ocean could prove to be crucial in either maintaining or altering this situation.

To begin with the United States did not have any direct interest in the Indian Ocean. It was actually induced by Britain to get a foothold in these waters. The British Foreign Office convinced the State Department about the importance of Pakistan as the inner circle of Western defence in the strategic Persian Gulf region and the southern belly of the Soviet empire. The British were also apprehensive about Imperial security in case India opted out of the Commonwealth and became susceptible to Russian Influence.

This is however not to suggest that Americans were themselves not aware of importance of sea power. In fact, a leading American strategist Captain A.T. Mahan demonstrated in his work how the British Empire fought with its navy, and with its economic strength rose to become the empire that it was in the 18th-19th century. Mahan urged that America's prosperity if not survival depended on the powerful revival of sea power. According to him, great powers were those that maintained strong navies and merchant marines. He urged the US to give emphasis to its naval building programmes and provided a rationale for the American acquisition of port facilities throughout the world.[1]

The importance of Indian Ocean was highlighted in a big way by another prominent American strategist, Robert D. Kaplan. He argues that in the past it was in the Atlantic and Pacific theatres that the great wars of that era were lost and won. But in the 21st century this is going to fundamentally change, and the IOR would become central to American power. A number of countries of this region like India, Pakistan, China, Indonesia, Myanmar, Oman, Sri Lanka, Bangladesh and Tanzania represent a shift in global balance that cannot be ignored. According to him, the Indian Ocean area will be the true nexus of world power and conflict in the coming years. It is here that the fight for democracy, energy independence, and religious freedom would be lost or won, and it is here that American foreign policy must concentrate if America is to remain dominant in an ever-changing world.[2]

One of the foremost writers to express Indian perspective on the Indian Ocean and sea power was K.M. Panikkar. According to him, the "importance of the sea came to be recognised by the Indian rulers only when it was too late". Panikkar elucidates the conditions under which the Indian Navy had to develop: firstly, more symbolic as the Royal Indian Navy; secondly, as a force to take over the coastal duties; and thirdly, to create a naval tradition.[3] He argued that "while to other countries the Indian Ocean is only one of the important oceanic areas, to India it is a vital sea. Her lifelines are concentrated in that area, her freedom is dependent on the freedom of that water surface. No industrial development, no commercial growth, no stable political structure is possible for her unless her shores are protected".[4]

Top Indian leaders have also highlighted the importance of the Indian Ocean to Indian security and its economic prosperity. Pandit Nehru said, "History has shown that whatever power controls the Indian Ocean has, in the first instance, India's sea borne trade at her mercy and, in the second, India's very independence itself." Indira Gandhi too warned, "The Ocean has brought conquerors to India in the past. Today we find it churning with danger." She wanted all major powers to withdraw from the Indian Ocean out of concern for great power rivalry.

India along with other nations of the IOR wanted it to be Zone of Peace. A proposal to declare the Indian Ocean a Zone of Peace was introduced by Sri Lanka, which was unanimously adopted by the UN General Assembly in 1971. The General Assembly under UN Resolution 2832 (XXVI) of December 16, 1971, declared that the Indian Ocean "within limits to be determined, together with the air space above and the ocean floor subjacent thereto", to be designated for all time as a Zone of Peace. The proposal was subsequently also supported by the 113-member Non-Aligned Movement.[5] This approach then suited a non-aligned Third World country wanting to be economically self reliant. India of this period also wanted to distance itself from the British Raj, which had long been the central security provider in the Indian Ocean.

The context which gave rise to this Indian approach began to change in the 1990s as India moved on a path of economic globalization which also ended its military isolation. India's new maritime imperatives did not, however, translate into a vigorous national strategy. Its policy towards the Indian Ocean continued to be marked by a lack of coherence, political ambivalence, and continuation of a continentalist mindset. The top political leadership still had neither the time nor the inclination to lay out clear goals for the Indian Ocean or the maritime space beyond. India was however forced to take a close look on its maritime security as Chinese started developing their blue-water navy overcoming their earlier continentalist obsession.

The importance of the Indian Ocean is to a large measure because of the Sea Lanes of Communication (SLOCs) that pass through it. A major part of world's seaborne trade takes place through them. The energy resources required by the world's major economies pass through them. Moreover, the important centres of production of oil and gas – both offshore and onshore – are located around it. Besides, this region is also rich in fisheries and undersea minerals. These resources, in particular oil and gas reserves, have aroused and maintained the interest of the world's major and upcoming powers for their economic and strategic value.

A new struggle for dominance over the Indian Ocean has started with the rise of major economic powers in the Asia-Pacific that depend on energy imports to sustain their growth. In any case, it is in the interest of world economy that a free and uninterrupted flow of oil and goods is maintained through the ocean's SLOCs. To maintain peace and stability in this region, the world still relies on the US, but another emerging power, China does not want to depend on Americans for keeping the sea lanes secure. Besides, it also appears that the Chinese interests in this region have grown beyond just the protection of SLOCs. They are now also interested in the resources of Africa and power projection in the Indian Ocean. To serve these interests, China wants to engage closely with the Maldives. Though India does not treat the Indian Ocean – the only region and ocean of the world that is named after a single state, as "India's Ocean", the ongoing power politics in this region has significant implications for Indian security and strategic interests as well.

Maritime Challenges in the IOR

The IOR is rich in resources and major SLOCs pass through it, but it also faces immense maritime challenges. The most important issue that causes tension in the region is the attempt by major global powers to get a foothold in these waters for their economic, navigational, security, and strategic requirements. Besides this, there are also a number of other maritime challenges:

Protection of SLOCs

Most of the international trade is conducted through sea routes, and SLOCs form the lifeline of countries. With the growth in trade and commerce, seaborne trade is only expected to rise. However, this increase in trade also gives rise to a variety of threats like piracy, maritime terrorism, drug trafficking, gun-running, human smuggling, pollution, accidents, and inter-state conflicts. The best way to protect SLOCs is through extensive cooperation, but this cooperation is difficult to get, as SLOCs arouse different response strategies amongst different people. While an economist might view SLOCs as the shortest and most economical travel distance between two destinations, a military analyst views SLOCs as a maritime instrument of power, and maritime geography becomes the pivot on which forces must be deployed. Similarly, some countries consider multilateral cooperation on SLOCs as infringement on their sovereignty. This necessitates comprehensive strategies to protect sea lanes which encompass differing perceptions and national interests of concerned states.[6]

The Indian Ocean is home to important SLOCs and maritime choke points. A large volume of international long-haul maritime cargo from the Persian Gulf, Africa, and Europe transits through this ocean. A significant part of this cargo is energy products – mainly oil and gas. These energy products often transit through the Strait of Hormuz and any disruption there could cut off Gulf supplies to the major world economies. Similarly, the closure of the Strait of Malacca can seriously threaten the economies of Southeast Asia and the energy intensive economies of China and Japan. An alternative route goes through the Sunda and the Lombok Straits, but that could also be vulnerable due to political instability in Indonesia. Due to the geostrategic importance of Malacca Strait to almost all the South and Southeast Asian countries, any maritime contingency in this traffic congested region would have profound security ramifications.

The SLOCs are critically important for the energy-intensive economies of India, China, and Japan. Their consumption of energy is only expected to rise which makes it imperative to protect SLOCs. Most of their imported oil originates in West Asia and passes through Hormuz. These supply lines could also be disrupted in the event of a political turmoil in the West Asia. In the past, it has been seen that on most occasions these disruptions happened because of the political reasons and were not market driven.

Piracy

The Indian Ocean also has the problem of piracy. In the past the Malacca Strait, the Bay of Bengal and the Arabian Sea were the affected areas. The problem of piracy is often linked with other forms of maritime disorders like narco-terrorism and human smuggling.

The increasing instances of piracy have threatened the peaceful use of navigational routes by vessels of all nations. Somali pirates have expanded their area of activity from the territorial waters of Somalia to the high seas. Using "mother ships" as extensions of their mainland facilities, Somali pirates use smaller high-speed motor boats to attack seafaring vessels, cargo, and cruise ships. Their recent attacks took place in the Gulf of Aden, which is very close to South Asia. These acts of piracy have resulted in increasing insurance rates and transportation costs for shipping companies as vessels have to seek alternative routes to avoid the pirate-infested area, usually sailing around South Africa, which is a much longer route, incurring higher expenditures. While there is concern about piracy in the Malacca Strait, much of it is under control because of the collective vigilance exercised by Indonesia, Malaysia, and Singapore. The Indian Navy has already had to intervene in more than one incident in the Gulf of Aden. Following an attack by Somali pirates on a Chinese ship off the coast of Yemen, China sent naval ships to the region to serve as maritime escorts. The effective handling of the problem of piracy requires that law enforcement agencies of various states cooperate or else the problem might spin out of control.

Maritime Terrorism

In the post-9/11 era the possibility of maritime terrorism has increased. When the US was fighting the war against terror in Afghanistan an effort was made to prevent Osama Bin Laden and Al Qaeda operatives from escaping via the sea or terrorising the maritime arena. Some of the terror organisations in and around the Indian Ocean are known to possess merchant fleets of various types. An entire flotilla of the Liberation Tigers of Tamil Eelam (LTTE) is known to have engaged in dubious maritime trade. The November 2008 terrorist attacks in Mumbai, India, point to the urgent need for the recognition of the maritime dimension of the security threat linked to terrorism.

An adjunct to maritime terrorism is drug trafficking. This illegal trade has a huge profit margin and is the most lucrative means of generating funds to fuel ever-growing terrorist activities and insurgencies around the region. Drug trafficking also has symbiotic relationship with gunrunning. Gunrunning by sea is by far the safest means for transferring arms and ammunition around the world.

Security against Mining

Mining of waters is one of the cheapest ways to conduct maritime warfare. Mines may be laid by seaborne or airborne vessels. Civilian aircraft or vessels may carry out mining operations, which can even be perpetrated by non-state actors to a limited extent. It is not even necessary to carry out actual mining operations and ships could be deterred from entering into an "affected" channel or strait by simply running a disinformation campaign about the laying of a minefield. A number of ships were damaged by the mines that were laid in the Persian Gulf in 1987 and the Red Sea in 1984. A concerted international effort was required to undertake minesweeping operations to clean up the area. The mining in a constricted area like the Malacca Straits has the potential to create havoc on international merchant shipping.[7]

Natural Disasters and Oil-related Environmental Disasters

The IOR region is also prone to natural disasters. The devastation caused by the December 2004 tsunami in India, Indonesia, Sri Lanka, and Thailand illustrates how far-reaching maritime catastrophes can be. The tsunami badly affected the fishing industry of Sri Lanka. Of the 30,000 people who died in the tsunami, a majority were fishers and their family members. A large number of fisher communities were displaced because of lost housing and coastal infrastructure. The industry has now recovered due to international help to a great extent, but the threat of future natural disasters remains.

Oil-related disasters at sea can create havoc with the ecology in the maritime environment and have the potential to affect maritime security. Major oil spills or wrecks of oil tankers at narrow approaches to harbours and choke points can seriously affect the flow of merchant shipping traffic.

Absence of a Unified Trans-Oceanic Community in the IOR

The IOR has failed to emerge as a unified trans-oceanic community though the nations are linked together through this ocean. They have considerable difference in their economic and military capabilities. While some of the nations like India, Australia and South Africa each have blue water naval capability and a booming economy, some of the smaller island nations are quite behind. Hence, a convergence on security interests has been difficult to achieve.

The IOR countries however require cooperative mechanisms to successfully deal with challenges posed by maritime issues. They have to deal with a range of issues that include navigational issues, security challenges, maritime threats posed by state and non-state actors and non-traditional security threats like marine pollution and coastal degradation, the impacts of global warming and natural disasters. Similar cooperation would also be needed for exploitation of resources like fisheries and seabed mining.

The cooperative mechanisms are required at bilateral, regional, and eventually global levels so that they can effectively deal with problems depending upon their nature. To deal with issues like fisheries, India and Sri Lanka and Sri Lanka and Maldives have mechanisms at bilateral levels. However, bilateral mechanisms are not sufficient to deal with major issues in the region though they can help reduce irritants among two or three nations. For instance, larger security issues like terrorism and piracy must be addressed on the regional and multi-lateral level and in a collaborative manner.

The region succeeded in creating its first cooperative mechanism in March 1997, in Mauritius when it formed the Indian Ocean Rim Association for Regional Cooperation (IOR-ARC) with the objective to boost economic cooperation. It was subsequently renamed as Indian Ocean Rim Association (IORA) and has now begun to address maritime security issues. In June 1997, another economic community (EC) comprising of Bangladesh, India, Myanmar (Burma), Sri Lanka, and Thailand (BIMST), the BIMST-EC was launched in the region. This was later renamed as the Bay of Bengal Initiative for Multi-Sectoral Technical and Economic Cooperation (BIMSTEC). This organisation has also not taken off in a major way and appears ill-equipped to handle maritime challenges. The other important organisation is the Indian Ocean Naval Symposium (IONS). This is a 35-member Indian Ocean security apparatus which facilitates exchange of views among the naval professionals to evolve common understanding of maritime security issues in the region. The exercises held under the name, "Milan" (confluence) bring together the navies from India's extended neighbourhood of Southeast Asia, Australia, and New Zealand. In the Milan exercises that were held in the 2014 at Port Blair in the Andaman & Nicobar Islands in the Bay of Bengal, 17 navies with 15 ships participated.[8]

Though IORA, IONS, and Milan are successful models of maritime cooperation, they have generally shied away from addressing hard security issues which appear in the region in two forms. First, there is gradual increase in naval power of the littoral states. Second, this region also has the presence of extra-regional powers that are forward deployed in the Indian Ocean to support national strategic and economic interests. Thus, the Indian Ocean emerges as a region where there is possibility of both cooperation as well as competition.[9]

In the IOR, the United States is seen as a strategic anchor. Its presence is however perceived differently. Some see it as a coercive power, whereas others consider it as security provider. The presence of the US in the IOR has been legitimised by some regional countries that have willingly created space for the country to correct security imbalances, challenge the hegemony of the dominant power, and ensure regional stability. The US Navy conducts joint naval exercises and shares intelligence with its alliance partners. This assures them of its political and diplomatic commitments. A section, however, also perceives the US as a remnant of the colonial past whose presence adds to insecurity.[10] In these circumstances, IORA, IONS, and Milan could explore confidence-building measures to preclude unnecessary naval standoffs.

Strategic Interests of the Major Indian Ocean Players

The Indian Ocean has always enjoyed a place of prominence in the global strategy and many regional and extra-regional actors have established and maintained a presence here to ensure their strategic interests. Among the regional players India, Australia, and South Africa are the strongest and have blue water navy. The Indian Navy has over 140 vessels. It has aircraft carriers, submarines, expeditionary platforms, and long-range maritime surveillance aircraft which are supported by a sophisticated network-centric capability including a dedicated military satellite. The combat capability of the Australian Navy is based on submarines, air defence destroyers, fighter jets, and long-range maritime patrol aircraft.

In the Arabian Gulf, Iran is another important regional military power. In recent times, Iran has also made deep forays into the Indian Ocean. Similarly, the Pakistan Navy has an impressive array of air, surface, and sub-surface capabilities. It has also emerged into a major force and is trying to enhance its capabilities further by sourcing eight Yuan-class submarines from China.

In Southeast Asia, Malaysia, Indonesia, and a number of other littoral states are strengthening their militaries. Malaysia is now focused more than ever before on the potential strategic importance of the Indian Ocean approaches to Peninsula Malaysia. The country apprehends some threat to its security because of its strategic location in the waterways of the South China Sea and Indian Ocean. To meet this possible security challenge, the Malaysian Navy has started construction of a new navy base and command centre at Langkawi. This is Malaysia's only port directly fronting the Indian Ocean. Similarly, Indonesia has also been establishing military infrastructure projects in the Ocean. Singapore monitors security situation on behalf of the US near the Straits.

Among the extra-regional powers, the United States is the most powerful military power in the IOR. It enjoys a number of port access and basing agreements with countries like Australia, Bahrain, India, Iraq, Kuwait, Oman, Pakistan, Qatar, Saudi Arabia, Singapore, Thailand, the United Arab Emirates (UAE), and Yemen. The US primarily projects its military power in the region through its navy. The US Navy gets support from the British Royal Navy which is also forward deployed in the Indian Ocean. It is also part of the 1971 Five Powers Defence Arrangement (FPDA). The piracy off the Somalia coast made the European Union take part in the security dynamics of the Indian Ocean. The Operation Atlanta in the Gulf of Aden was its first ever naval operation. The European power, France, though, does not consider itself an extra-regional power in the Indian Ocean, and its navy is forward deployed at Mayotte, Le Reunion, Djibouti, and Abu Dhabi.

Among the major extra-regional Asian powers, Japan and China are important as they are major consumers of energy. Generally, there is a tendency to underestimate Japan's military power especially its navy. In 2006, Japan had 16 submarines and 54 principal surface combatants (destroyers and frigates), and 109 Lockheed Orion P-3C antisubmarine warfare aircraft in various modes. Japan has forward deployed its maritime and air forces in the Indian Ocean that operate out of its military facilities in Djibouti. Japanese Maritime Self Defence Force (MSDF) destroyers and refuelling supply ships have been continually on-station in the Indian Ocean since November 2001. The MSDF ships were dispatched under the Anti-Terrorism Special Measures Law (2001), which has since been extended a number of times beyond its original two-year period of application.

The most important Asian power which has changed the power equation in the Indian Ocean is China. China's engagement in the Indian Ocean is through its naval task force (CTF 525), and since 2008, it has deployed 25 warships in 10 groups. After the fall of the Soviet Union, the successor state, Russia has also shown interest in the security dynamics of the Indian Ocean. The Russian Navy's show of 'flag' and 'presence' in the Indian Ocean reflects its ambition to engage in distant water operations. Likewise, the North Atlantic Treaty Organisation (NATO) has keenly observed the security dynamics in the Indian Ocean.

The Indian Ocean has been an important transit point for non-littoral powers. Russia needs it for maritime transit between Europe and Eastern Siberia. The energy hungry major East Asian powers like China and Japan need it for transit of vital flows of oil and gas. The Indian Ocean is also a major maritime trade route between East Asia and Europe. Moreover, the US Pacific Command (USPACOM) with its headquarters in Hawaii looks at the Indian Ocean as a strategic back door into the Gulf for the US.

Though a number of countries have deployed their naval and military power in the Indian Ocean, it would be useful to consider the strategic interests of some major powers that can significantly influence the strategic environment of this region.

Indian Interests in the Indian Ocean

Though India is predominantly a continental power, it occupies a central position in the Indian Ocean region. This fact greatly influences India's security environment. The accessibility of the Indian Ocean to the fleets of the world's most powerful states, rising religious radicalism and extremism on the shores of the ocean and in its hinterland, the oil wealth of the Persian Gulf, the proliferation of conventional military power and nuclear weapons among the region's states and smooth accessibility of key straits are some of the important security considerations of India.

A number of countries of this region are afflicted with poverty, backwardness, fundamentalism, terrorism or internal insurgency. There are lingering territorial and maritime disputes and most of the conflicts since the end of the Cold War have also taken place in or around this region. In this kind of situation, it is only natural that India believes that their security would be best guaranteed by enlarging its security perimeter and by achieving a position of influence in the Indian Ocean region. From the point of view of maritime security India's security perimeter would extend from the Strait of Malacca to the Strait of Hormuz and from the coast of Africa to the western shores of Australia. It would be only desirable for India that it takes a leadership role in the region and becomes the predominant influence. Thus one of the strategic objectives of India would be to emerge as a regional power in short term while its long term goal could be to achieve great power status on an Asian and perhaps even at global scale.

India's second goal in the region could be to ensure that present and potential role of external powers in the Indian Ocean does not jeopardize Indian security. As has been pointed out by the Indian Maritime Doctrine all major powers are likely to seek a toehold in the Indian Ocean in this century. It expects Japan, the EU, and China, and a reinvigorated Russia to show presence in these waters either independently or through politico-security arrangements. It also notices "an increasing tendency of extra regional powers of military intervention in [IO] littoral countries to contain what they see as a conflict situation."It further says that the battle for oil dominance and its control in the littoral and hinterland are factors that are likely to have long-term impact on the overall security environment in the Indian Ocean region.

In near future India's concern about the external powers seem related to China and the US though the recent development in India-US ties has moderated India's sensitivity to the US presence in the Arabian Sea. India now also seems to have moved away from the traditional rhetoric of non-alignment and the Indian Ocean as a 'zone of peace.' Malabar exercises have further boosted their confidence in each other, where Japan has also now become a regular participant.

Thirdly, India is also concerned by the threat posed by Pakistan which has become the epicenter of world terrorism. The 26/11 terror attacks on Mumbai had originated from that country. The fourth motive of India in this region is to ensure its energy security. India is the fourth largest economy of the world which is almost 70 percent dependent on foreign oil and this dependence is only likely to increase in future. Moreover, India also has to protect its offshore oil and gas fields.

Finally, there are also important commercial reasons to pursue a robust Indian Ocean strategy. India's other trade and commerce is dependent on the Indian Ocean. The maritime arc from the Gulf through the Straits of Malacca to the Sea of Japan is the equivalent of the New Silk Route and total trade on this arc is U.S. $1,800 billion. Besides, large number of Indians live in the Gulf and Arab countries. Their remittances play an important role in the Indian economy.

Keeping these interests in view, India is pursuing a variety of policies aimed at improving its strategic situation. It is forging a web of partnerships with certain littoral states and major external powers to increase its influence in the region. These partnerships take the shape of trade agreements, direct investment, military exercises, aid funds, energy cooperation and infrastructure building.

India's Sea Power

To supplement its diplomatic and political initiatives India is also focusing on its growing military capability. The objective of these forces would be to keep Chinese navy out of the Indian Ocean in case of need. India would also like to project power at various choke points in the Indian Ocean. It may also be interested in power projection in the South China Sea.

India's sea power had a slow start. After independence, the first Naval Plan papers envisaged the role of be Navy to 'safeguard her shipping on the high seas from interference in war; to ensure that supplies can both reach and leave India by sea in all circumstances; to keep open her ports and coastal shipping routes; to prevent any enemy landing on her shores; and to support the Army in any operations which may be required in the furtherance of the national policy.

But this plan could not be implemented because of India's hostile neighbours Pakistan which started a war on Kashmir in 1947-48 and because of budgetary constraints. However, by 1961 the Indian navy had acquired a number of major warships. India bought its first four submarines from the Soviet Union which were inducted in the Indian navy from 1967 to 1969. They were sourced from the Soviet Union because at that time it was the only country willing to meet the Indian navy's increasing requirements. These requirements were driven by the recommendations post the 1962 Sino-Indian war that the Navy should have a fleet in both the Arabian Sea and Bay of Bengal with 'a force level of 138 ships'. These acquisitions by the Indian navy was considered appropriate to meet the country's security specifically and that of the IOR in general. Indian naval strategists, however, now envisage the navy as a three-carrier force—one on each coast and one in reserve—by 2015–20.

India's maritime prowess was perhaps recognised for the first time in

1971 war when Indian navy was used effectively in war with Pakistan. Subsequently, the Indian navy also played a stabilising role in 1988 when it was used to avert the coup in the Maldives against Gayoom.

In the post-Cold War era, both India and China witnessed rapid economic growth which once again brought focus on the Indian Ocean region to protect the maritime trade. The trade in energy (oil) was especially important. Hence it became necessary to ensure a secure maritime environment. This period once again saw expansion in India's naval capabilities. India has a longstanding intention of adding a sea-based leg to its nuclear posture. Presently, India is trying to equip its navy and air force with nuclear capabilities that could be employed in a contingency.

The US Interests in the Indian Ocean

The US interest in the Indian Ocean increased during the Cold War period as it wanted to counter the influence of the former Soviet Union, which had occupied Afghanistan and enjoyed a special relationship with India. The former Soviet Union was also interested in Afghanistan because it had the potential to offer them access to warm water ports in the Indian Ocean. To make its presence permanent in the Indian Ocean, the United States in 1971 established its military base on the British island of Diego Garcia after signing a lease agreement with the United Kingdom in 1966. This lease expires in 2016 and could be renewed for another 20 years.[11] However, Britain is also under pressure to return these Chagos Islands to Mauritius.[12] Diego Garcia is the biggest island of the Chagos archipelago and is located close to the Maldives. One of the five ground antennas that comprise the US Global Positioning Satellite system is installed here.

During the Cold War period the route from Hawaii to the Indian Ocean along with American bases and facilities in the IOR, were important to the US Gulf strategy in a number of respects. It remains so even today. This route could be used as an important backup in case transit through Suez Canal is ever denied. It can also be used for deploying the US forces and equipment located in the west of continental US and in the Pacific into the Gulf. The naval base at Diego Garcia gives the US ability to quickly deploy forces either through ship or by air. Moreover, this base can also be used by the B-52 bombers in case there is a need to undertake aerial bombardment. The US also profitably used the Indian Ocean, particularly the Arabian Sea, to launch ship-based ballistic missiles in both Gulf wars. Finally, Australia located at the other corner of the Indian Ocean has been providing vital listening, targeting, and monitoring facilities for the US forces.

During the Cold War period, the littoral powers viewed the strategic interests of outside powers somewhat differently. In this period, India was seen as having a pro-Soviet tilt which became more pronounced after the US Seventh Fleet moved into the Bay of Bengal during the India-Pakistan War of 1971. The steady escalation of the arms race and the competitive military presence in the region made India and some other nations of this region favour a "Zone of Peace" in the Indian Ocean.[13] This concept was not liked by the Western powers including the US who perceived it as favouring the former Soviet Union, and granting it the right to innocent passage but precluding the US warships from loitering and basing. However, efforts of this kind came to an end with the end of the Cold War.

In the post-Cold War period, too, the US has maintained a high level of interest in the IOR. Diego Garcia is still seen as crucial to furthering it. This base was further expanded, and in 2002, construction on new hangers for B-2 bombers was started and runways were extended.[14] Similarly, "Camp Justice", a facility designed to hold soldiers engaged in the "war on terror", and also believed to hold a prison for suspected terrorists, was approved and completed. Now with the new US policy of "pivot to Asia" the importance of Diego Garcia and the Indian Ocean has increased manifold.

Though the Indian Ocean has remained important for the US in the post-Cold War world, its relationship with many littoral countries and beyond has changed. Now the strategic scenario is completely different from what it was.

With respect to India, an increasing convergence in the Indian and American interests has been seen. Though the debate regarding the US presence in the Indian Ocean and its role is far from resolved, there is a greater realisation that the US is a predominant power in this region, and India will have to deal with it. However, Americans have also begun to see India as a prominent power in this region. With the disappearance of the Soviet threat, Americans now have no problem if India emerges as a regional power and plays its role in the regional security and in the IOR. The US probably wants to support this process by transferring technology either directly or through Israel. Both countries have now a number of common interests like fight against religious fundamentalism, illegal drug trafficking, and support for unrestricted navigation in the Indian Ocean and elsewhere. The signing of the nuclear deal even removed the last remaining hurdle. In recent years, both countries have developed a deep military-to-military relationship. Both sides signed a 10-year Defence Framework Agreement (DFA) in 2005 which was renewed in 2015 for another 10 years.[15]

The US is however also alive to the fact that this closeness does not necessarily mean that India has become its ally. India is also not likely to give up its relationships with other powers, especially Russia which has supported India's Arihant SSBN project.[16] Moreover, India is also likely to follow its principle of strategic autonomy.

The US policy towards India to a large measure is directed by the emergence of China as a major power. Americans want India to emerge as a major Asian military power so that it can help balance China's rise. Though India may not like to be used by the Americans in this role, presently it is hedging against China. On the other hand, though Americans are also not sure whether they can turn Indian into an ally, they are hopeful that their friendship with India would unsettle the power equation for China which is rising rapidly in military capability. They also believe that a powerful India will be a more benign and pro-US presence in the region than a powerful China. Moreover, if the US were to refuse India what it wants in strategic parity with the Nuclear 5, then other countries, such as Russia, would.

In present times, Washington's IOR strategy is based on three imperatives – maintaining the Indian Ocean as a secure highway for international commerce, particularly between the oil-rich Gulf states and economically dynamic East Asia, avoiding regional conflict on issues of strategic choke points in the IOR (Strait of Hormuz and the Malacca Strait), and dealing with Sino-Indian competition in the IOR.[17] The US

Defence Department's document, *Strategic Choices and Management Review* (July 2013) has stressed the need for the US to develop an Indian Ocean policy on the basis of building coalitions with regional allies like Australia, Japan, and the Philippines, and partners like Vietnam and India. Washington is currently promoting an 'Indo-Pacific' concept, which connects the Indian and Pacific Oceans as part of its approach towards the IOR.

Strategic Interests of Australia in the IOR

Australia is an island continent and its western coast faces the Indian Ocean. The improving relationship between India and the US also has its impact on India-Australia relationship where strategic convergence seems to be increasing. Since Australia is an island continent, most of its trade is seaborne. Like India, Australia also wants to keep trades free and secure for the enormous flows of energy and other traded goods that pass across it. Australia is fast developing into an energy superpower with substantial exports in coal and natural gas. It also has significant naval presence in the Indian Ocean and wants to enhance maritime security in the Indian Ocean together with India where both have "key strategic interests to manage".[18]

In the 1990s Australia attempted to establish an Indian Ocean cooperative framework. It also sees itself as having a role and say in broader Indian Ocean security concerns and cooperative architecture. In this regard, Canberra sees the future triangular relationship between China, India and the US as vital.

Japan's Interests in the Indian Ocean Region (IOR)

Japan's primary interests in the Indian Ocean region (IOR) are related to the protection of Sea Lanes of Communication (SLCOs) that pass through it. This is the region through which the Red Sea path to Europe, and North Africa traverses. Moreover, Japan is also greatly dependent on the Middle Eastern oil for its energy needs.

In the past, Japan has been dependent on the security umbrella provided by the US. But as the US security dominance declines and the security environment in the IOR becomes uncertain with the entry of

China, Japanese concerns have increased. Japan is also concerned about the terrorism and piracy off the coast of Somalia in the Gulf of Aden that can affect its trade and commerce. Finally, as the IOR is plagued with disasters, Japan would also like to play a role in disaster relief in littoral states. Besides, it would also be interested in protection of its ex-patriot citizens.

In the Indian Ocean Japan views India's military power as maximizer of Japan's security interests. It takes Indian naval power as counterbalance to China's naval power. There is also some strategic divergence in India and Japan. For security purposes, Japan gives primacy to U.S.-Japan Alliance. On the other hand, India gives primacy to its strategic autonomy. It prefers a multi-polar world and selective cooperation with the US, Australia and Japan.

China's Interests and Activities in the Indian Ocean

China's interests and activities in the Indian Ocean are largely motivated by its increasingly important supplies of energy that need to transit that region. China however also sees itself as a long-term competitor of the US and India in the region. It fears that its vital oil and gas supplies could be cut off during times of rising tension or actual war with India and/or the US. This could happen at two choke points – the Straits of Hormuz and to a lesser degree the Straits of Malacca. To meet with this challenge, it is trying to increase its naval presence at the choke points. It is also trying to develop alternative routes through Gwadar and Myanmar. In fact, China National Petroleum Corporation, the nation's biggest oil and gas company, has already started trial operations at a crude pipeline in Myanmar that could shorten the time for shipments to reach refineries.[19]

The US is the most dominant player in the Indian Ocean. It has a well-defined strategy to maintain its pre-eminence. The US maritime strategy of the 1980s envisioned a war at sea won by sea control.[20] China however does not want to depend on the protection provided by the US. It is aware of the US interest in the Indian Ocean and has tried to establish its presence in the region, initially through links with Pakistan (because of the strained relations that both countries have with India) and, more recently, with Sri Lanka, Bangladesh and Maldives. China's efforts to gain a foothold in the Indian Ocean are also seen by many as an attempt to assert itself.

Emergence of Chinese Maritime Security Interests

With the growth of Chinese economic and military power there has been a continuous evolution of their national interests. As core interests of China keep expanding, its security requirements are also expanding. China has been moving away from Mao Zedong and Zhou En Lai's "People's War" doctrine biased toward land-based wars and land-based forces to sea-based forces.[21] The Chinese Navy, according to the Defence White Paper of 2006, aims at a "gradual extension of the strategic depth for offshore defensive operations and enhancing its capabilities in integrated maritime operations and nuclear counter-attacks".[22] The Chinese intention to expand the capabilities of its navy so that it can operate abroad also came out in the 2013 Defence White Paper which talked of "protecting national maritime rights and interests" and "armed forces providing reliable support for China's interests overseas". Along with its evolving national interests, China has also kept expanding its defence budget and most importantly the budget of its navy. China now has the second-highest defence expenditure in the world.[23]

The ambition of China to become a maritime power comes out quite clearly in its latest 2015 Defence White Paper:

> The seas and oceans bear on the enduring peace, lasting stability and sustainable development of China. The traditional mentality that land outweighs sea must be abandoned, and great importance has to be attached to managing the seas and oceans and protecting maritime rights and interests. It is necessary for China to develop a modern maritime military force structure commensurate with its national security and development interests, safeguard its national sovereignty and maritime rights and interests, protect the security of strategic SLOCs and overseas interests, and participate in international maritime cooperation, so as to provide strategic support for building itself into a maritime power.[24]

China now clearly identifies the US and Japan as security threats. The 2015 Defence White Paper talks of the US "rebalancing" strategy and its enhanced military presence and military alliances in Asia Pacific region. It also notes the Japanese attempt "to overhaul its military and security policies" dodging the post-war mechanism.

This Defence White Paper also talks of "the growth of China's national interests", and points out that Chinese national security is now more vulnerable "to international and regional turmoil, terrorism, piracy, serious natural disasters and epidemics, and the security of overseas interests concerning energy and resources, strategic SLOCs, as well as institutions, personnel and assets abroad, has become an imminent issue". China is now alive to "the country's growing strategic interests", and wants the armed forces to "effectively secure China's overseas interests".

To meet this requirement the People's Liberation Army Navy (PLAN) is now going to gradually shift its focus from "offshore waters defence" to the combination of "offshore waters defence" with "open seas protection", and build a combined, multifunctional, and efficient marine combat force structure.

China is reluctant to depend on the US naval power to keep sea lanes open in Indian Ocean through which 80 per cent of its oil passes. It has decided to boost its own naval power at "choke points" along the sea routes from the Persian Gulf to the South China Sea. China has deployed its Jin-class submarines at a submarine base near Sanya on the southern tip of Hainan Island in South China Sea.[25]

China is not looking for a subsidiary role under the leadership of US military, rather it wants its armed forces to "continue to foster a new model of military relationship with the US armed forces that conforms to the new model of major-country relations between the two countries, strengthen defence dialogues, exchanges and cooperation, and improve the CBM mechanism for the notification of major military activities as well as the rules of behaviour for safety of air and maritime encounters, so as to strengthen mutual trust, prevent risks and manage crises".[26]

With this objective China is now expanding their navy. It is building a maritime force structure around aircraft carrier.[27] The Chinese Navy is now only behind the US and Russia and is superior to the Indian Navy in both qualitative and quantitative terms.[28] Traditionally, it has been a coastal force, but now with the increase in China's economic might and its interests, it has now acquired maritime orientation and wants to project power into the Indian Ocean. It has been suggested that soon the Chinese would be in a position to challenge the Americans. Clearly, the goal of PLA's modernisation is not limited to just capturing Taiwan.[29]

China's sophisticated submarine fleet is increasing. Chinese submarines are now making forays into the Indian Ocean. They have docked twice at the Colombo port in Sri Lanka and once in Gwadar. India had protested the presence of Chinese submarines in Sri Lanka when it docked first but despite the National Security Advisor (NSA), Ajit Doval's warning to the Lankan Defence Secretary, Gotabaya Rajapaksa, that any presence of a Chinese submarine in Sri Lanka would be unacceptable to India, Sri Lankans let a Chinese submarine dock once again.[30] China's Defence Ministry however defended its decision to dock submarines at the Colombo port and stated that "it was an international common practice for navy submarine(s) to stop for refuelling and crew refreshment at an overseas port".[31] Clearly, the sending of submarines to the Indian Ocean is not for protection against piracy. Actually, the Chinese are trying to test their ability to deploy forces in distant places.[32] This kind of long-distance deployment of Chinese submarines could also pose challenge to the US pacific fleet.

The long-distance deployment of submarines also makes it imperative for the Chinese to look for naval bases and access points. They are doing this along the crucial choke points to serve their economic interests and to enhance strategic presence in the region. China is looking to set up a naval base in the strategically located Djibouti on the Horn of Africa. It was Djibouti President, Ismail Omar Guelleh, who himself declared that discussions were underway with the Chinese for a naval base at Obock in the former French colony, a country the US already has a base in.[33]

The naval base in Djibouti, which overlooks the narrow Bab al-Mandeb straits, is part of China's larger Indian Ocean plans. This base would also prove useful when China starts implementing its Maritime Silk Road project and would pose challenge to India in its own backyard. A Pentagon report on China's military says that Beijing wants to expand its access to logistics in the Indian Ocean and would likely establish several access points in this area in the next 10 years.[34] These arrangements could take the form of agreements for refuelling, replenishment, crew rest, and low-level maintenance.

It is only expected that China would leverage its enhanced maritime presence in the future to emerge as a regional hegemon or even a superpower. Chinese diplomacy has been successful in wooing South Asian states. It has built container ports in Bangladesh at Chittagong and in Sri Lanka at Hambantota. It is suspected that at Hambantota Chinese have also constructed some naval facility.[35] Chinese have also acquired a terminal for 30 years in the Colombo port.[36]

It is difficult to explain the construction of these ports and facilities around India's periphery by China on purely economic and commercial grounds. Most of these ports are not viable unless they serve non-economic purposes. The deep sea port at Gwadar and Hambantota will allow Chinese to monitor Indian and the US naval activity in the region. If we take into account this aspect of Chinese ventures, then this also means containment of India and a challenge to the US military power.

As the Sino-Indian relationship remains largely competitive, the growing maritime strength of China would serve to confine India within South Asia with the help of its key allies like Pakistan. China's first priority would always be to protect its energy security interests, by securing the SLOCs that spread from the Gulf to the South China Sea. In the short and medium term, China may persist with its 'harmonious sea' approach keeping in view the superior US maritime power and huge strategic advantage bestowed on India because of its geographical location. For the time being it might not adopt a military approach and push for 'constructive engagement' in the IOR between the three powers – the US, China, and India – and concentrate on achieving 'greater space' in the IOR by way of promoting maritime security cooperation with the Indian Ocean littorals.[37] It is also possible that China may try to rebalance its ties with India as it is highly unlikely that India would give up its strategic autonomy.[38]

At present China would be happy to play a greater role in the region, protecting and advancing its interests, especially Chinese commerce, as well as countering India. The Chinese presence in Indian Ocean would significantly expand China's strategic depth in India's backyard and is likely to reduce the manoeuvrability of Indian Navy. In the long term, with continuous accretion of maritime power, China may also like to project its own power.[39] Beijing is also actively working to create alternative energy supply routes, safe from the US and Indian challenges.

China and the Maritime Silk Route

The maritime arc from the Gulf through the Malacca Straits up to the Sea of Japan is like New Silk Route. The value of trade on commerce on this route is estimated to be around US $ 1800 billion. China is planning to create huge infrastructural network in this region which they claim is similar to old Silk Route network. Though the Chinese Silk Route project has both overland and maritime components, this region will get its latter part. The maritime component is known as Maritime Silk Road (MSR). In ancient times, the MSR was a maritime trade route for trading of silk between China and South Asia, West Asia, Europe, and North Africa.

In the MSR project the immediate target of Chinese are the South East Asian nations with whom they have thriving trade and economic relationship. If the Chinese have to realise their 'China dream' then they need to nurture this relationship further which is facing difficulty because of the Chinese assertion in the South China Sea. With this objective China is pushing the MSR as a soft-power projection in the region to enhance its trade ties. Now Chinese claim they want to share their development dividend with the Association of Southeast Asian Nations (ASEAN) through the MSR.

In this sense, the proposed MSR project appears to be a strategic priority for China. To sell this project top Chinese leaders including President Xi Jinping and Premier Li have toured the ASEAN region extensively. During his visit to Malaysia and Indonesia in October 2013, President Xi Jinping underscored the 'shared destiny' of China and ASEAN members and invited them to join China to build a 'new maritime silk road'. It was claimed that it would help accelerate economies of the regional countries. Xi even proposed setting up a China-ASEAN Maritime Cooperation Fund to augment maritime-related projects being undertaken by the ASEAN member countries through capacity building.

However, it looks unlikely that the south East Asian countries would agree to the Chinese proposal regarding MSR so easily. The nature of trade in present times is different from what it was during the ancient times.

Earlier the route was used for the import of precious stone, wood, and spices, but today it would be used for oil and gas, which is directly connected to the energy security of not one but many countries. Moreover, the new emerging security architecture in South East Asia had led to an increased arms build-up, and the assertiveness of new regional powers has further complicated the regional military balance, which is bound to create hindrance in the path of MSR project.[40]

The ASEAN countries are also not enthusiastic about the MSR project because there is no clarity about the management of the fund, Chinese involvement in these projects, and public-private partnership. They also suspect Chinese intentions and are concerned about their security.

China has however received good response to MSR project from a number of countries in the Indian Ocean particularly the small island states who are constrained due to lack of expertise and finances.[41] Some of these countries also think that by bringing in China they can balance India and the US.

The proposed MSR could offer some opportunities for India which suffers from technological gaps in its maritime infrastructure. It could harness Chinese capability to construct high-quality ships, build world-class ports, etc. This will also help India-ASEAN maritime connectivity initiative which is languishing due to lack of infrastructure. In the past, however, Chinese companies have been barred from participation in India's maritime infrastructure projects due to security concerns. Before agreeing to participate in the MSR project, India will have to weigh its strategic implications which are going to be grave and bring China in a big way in the IOR.

China, on the other hand, stands to benefit from the MSR project in a number of ways. It would help China to dispel the notion of 'string of pearls' strategy, legitimise its engagement in Gwadar and other maritime infrastructure projects along the MSR. China currently fears that the US is trying to contain it by roping in Indian Ocean littorals within an 'Indo-Pacific' framework. However, some people also suggest that the Chinese MSR project is a refurbished Chinese plan to contain India using Pakistan and other nations of the Indian Ocean.[42]

The MSR is the Chinese effort to woo the IOR littorals through economic and other means. It is trying to build infrastructure in these littorals which also helps in its 'going global' strategy. It also helps Chinese economy which is facing some sluggishness and growth rates are hovering around seven per cent. Major Chinese corporates involved in infrastructural development work have lot of idle capacity which could be used in the MSR project. This could also revive Chinese economy which is having overcapacity in commodity production. Now the export of infrastructural projects could be another viable alternative and give China another round of economic growth and strategic advantage.

The proposal of China to develop a maritime silk route is to advance its strategic interests, become a maritime power, and also to undermine American attempts to woo Indian Ocean littorals in an economic framework.

China's Seabed Mining Forays in the IOR

The seabed of the Indian Ocean is rich in deposit of mineral resources. China's hunger for resources and its desire to become a maritime power has made the country explore the possibility of exploiting the resources available at seabed.

China actively took part in the 1970s in the UN-led discussions on seabed resource exploitation regime. At that time however it did not possess technological capability to exploit seabed resources. Subsequently, for seabed exploration and exploitation of resources, it formed a nodal agency called the China Ocean Mineral Resources Research and Development Association (COMRA). In 2001, China obtained mining rights for polymetallic nodule and in 2002, polymetallic sulfide deposits in the Southwestern Indian Ocean.

COMRA signed another agreement with the International Seabed Authority in 2011 that covered 10,000 sq. km of sea surface for research. Following this the Chinese started diving operations in the Indian Ocean in January 2015.[43] For this purpose, they used the submersible called Jiaolong whose primary task was to gather geological data, carry out assessment of seabed resources, and record biodiversity for exploration and mining.

China however still faces a number of technological challenges to develop undersea exploration and extraction systems and equipment. It is difficult for them to overcome this problem by importing specialised equipment from external sources. A majority of the "geophysical surveying instruments on the international market are not allowed to be sold to China" amidst fears that these highly sensitive sub-sea sensors could be used by the Chinese Navy to develop underwater detection system particularly for the submarines.[44]

It is also feared that Jiaolong could potentially be used to monitor submarine cables which carry nearly 99 per cent of digital data and crisscross the Indian Ocean. The undersea cables are prone to covert tapping and in the past, there have been a number of incidents when undersea cables were targeted. The 'Five Eyes Alliance' (comprising the United States, Canada, Britain, Australia, and New Zealand) is designed for eavesdropping on the network of cables which carry global phone calls and Internet traffic.

Jiaolong can also possibly monitor maritime and naval activity in the Indian Ocean. It could be used to protect its SLOCs. Jiaolong can also monitor the US, UK, France, and Indian nuclear submarine activity by trailing their radioactive signature. It is quite possible that China could use the Jiaolong beyond its scientific utility and for supporting the Chinese Navy's maritime strategy.

Possibly to overcome the technological challenges in undersea exploration China, ahead of Prime Minister Narendra Modi's visit to Beijing in May 2015, proposed cooperation with India on deep seabed mining in the Indian Ocean.[45] The Chinese argued that as both countries are at the same level in technology they should cooperate. However, the Chinese proposal to share technical knowledge of the seabed has always been seen with suspicion given the fears that China would obtain sensitive underwater data which could be used for its submarine operations.[46]

India's Attempt to Reinvigorate Policy towards the IOR

India believes that its maritime security can be best guaranteed by enlarging its security perimeter in the IOR and by achieving a position of influence in this region. Thus, it is hardly surprising that India has been participating in international forums like IORA and IONS. It has been participating in naval exercises like Malabar and Milan.

India's southern neighbours – Sri Lanka and the Maldives – however showed some signs of drifting away from its co-operative and advisory framework. This was especially evident after the Fourth Elam War (2006-09) in Sri Lanka and since the controversial transfer of power in the Maldives on February 7, 2012. At the same time, China has been getting close to these states in terms of strategic, economic, political, and cultural engagements. China however is yet to make a security-related move despite its growing commercial influence. India has responded to this increased thrust of China in the Indian Ocean by stepping up efforts to improve bilateral ties with Indian Ocean littorals. It wants to tell these nations that if they participate in a multi-lateral framework with India their physical security would be better taken care of. With this objective, India along with Sri Lanka and the Maldives had started the Trilateral Cooperation in Maritime Security in October 2011 when they held their first NSA-level Trilateral Meeting on Maritime Security Cooperation in Maldives.

Tri-Nation Maritime Agreement

In the next meeting that was held in July 2013 in Colombo, the three countries agreed on a roadmap for cooperation in maritime security in the following three categories of activities:

- Initiatives to enhance Maritime Domain Awareness through access to systems run under the aegis of the International Maritime Organisation (IMO), such as Long Range Identification and Tracking (LRIT) services and sharing of Automatic Identification System (AIS) data.
- Training and capacity building initiatives in areas of Maritime Domain Awareness, Search and Rescue, and Oil Pollution Response.
- Joint activities including trilateral exercises, maintaining lines of communication on illegal maritime activities, formulation of marine oil pollution response contingency plans and cooperation in legal and policy issues related to piracy.[47]

The trilateral agreement on maritime cooperation, called the 'outcome document', is meant to pool resources and share data in the region for better control over the territorial waters and detect suspicious movements.[48] The agreement brings Sri Lanka and the Maldives into Indian identification and tracking systems and also provides regular messaging regarding the lines of communication. The agreement may not give India preferential treatment in other country's Exclusive Economic Zones (EEZs), but it will provide the country critical information and monitoring advantages.[49] The agreement also provides possibility to expand the grouping.

Moreover, the agreement can take the shape of an inclusive security scheme and include other smaller nations in the neighbourhood, which also suffer from resource-crunch of the kind required to protect their expanding EEZ under the United Nations Convention on the Law of the Sea (UNCLOS) negotiations and geo-strategic security. Some other countries whose concerns and interests coincide with those of India, Maldives, and Sri Lanka are Mauritius and Seychelles. However, it's too early to say that it would emerge as a regional grouping that would render extra-territorial power-play ineffective.

The trilateral agreement could be seen as India's effort to play an enhanced role in the region to ensure maritime security. It enables India to continue its traditional role in the region to patrol and safeguard the EEZs of its southern neighbours, and keep the Indian Navy and its security apparatus informed about what is happening in its southern neighbourhood.

The progress of the agreement however still remains hostage to the development of bilateral relationship between India and Sri Lanka and India and the Maldives. Any increase in tension with these countries would make implementation of the agreement difficult. The consequence of even an interim reversal, if not an outright failure, could be disastrous for the maritime security in the region.

India's five-fold Framework for Maritime Engagement in the IOR

India now seems to have stepped up efforts to increase its influence in the IOR. Prime Minister Narendra Modi has visited a host of Indian Ocean states that included Mauritius, Seychelles, and Sri Lanka. His visit to the Maldives was cancelled on the last minute due to domestic political developments in that country which vitiated the environment inside the country as well as internationally.

These visits indicated that the Indian Ocean littoral is now at the top of India's policy priorities. In Mauritius, Modi laid out a five-fold framework for India's maritime engagement with the Indian Ocean littoral.[50] The first principle states that India would do whatever is necessary to secure its mainland and island territories and defend its maritime interests. After the November 2008 Mumbai terror attacks, Delhi is now acutely conscious of the potential terrorist attacks coming via the sea. At the same time, Delhi has also been deeply aware of the growing strategic significance of the Indian Ocean in global politics. Delhi now wants to work for ensuring a safe, secure and stable Indian Ocean Region that is beneficial for all.

The second principle emphasises India's desire to deepen security cooperation with regional partners. India is now interested in elevating its close security partnerships with both Seychelles and Mauritius. In Seychelles, Modi announced the gift of a second Dornier aircraft for maritime monitoring, signed an agreement for conducting hydrographic surveys, and launched a coastal surveillance radar project. The radar initiative is part of an ambitious project to build a maritime domain awareness network across the Indian Ocean. It calls for the establishment of eight surveillance radars in Mauritius, eight in Seychelles, six in Sri Lanka, and ten in Maldives. These will be linked to over 50 sites on the Indian coast and connected to an integrated analysis center near Delhi. In Mauritius, Indian-made offshore patrol vessel Barracuda was commissioned in the presence of Indian Prime Minister that marked India's commitment to maritime capacity building in small island republics. Agreements to develop infrastructure for connectivity in the Assumption Island in the Seychelles and Aga Lega in Mauritius were announced. These are likely to strengthen the defense capabilities of the two republics and give India a valuable foothold at critical locations in South Western Indian Ocean.

The third principle talks about building multilateral cooperative maritime security in the Indian Ocean. India now wants to help strengthen regional mechanisms in combating terrorism and piracy and responding to natural disasters. India hopes that Mauritius, Seychelles and other countries will join the trilateral security initiative it already has with Maldives and Sri Lanka.

The fourth element of this new maritime policy is sustainable economic development. In Seychelles, the Indian Prime Minister announced a joint working group to expand cooperation on the "blue economy" that will increase littoral states' understanding of ecology, resources, and allow them to harness the ocean in a sustainable manner. India also demonstrated considerable sensitivity to climate change concerns in the island nations.

Finally, India also seems to be discarding its longstanding reluctance to cooperate with other major powers in the Indian Ocean. While the primary responsibility for peace and stability in these waters rests with Indian Ocean states, India has also now acknowledged the important role that the United States plays in the region through dialogue, exercises, economic partnerships, and capacity building efforts. Possibly being alive to this fact, now India and the US have also signed a broad framework for expanding cooperation in the Indian Ocean and Asia-Pacific.

It seems that India is now willing to take a larger responsibility for securing the Indian Ocean. It wants to promote regional mechanisms for collective security and economic integration. It is no longer averse to collaborate with the US to improve the security environment in the Indian Ocean region while being open to engaging China on maritime issues.

Maldives and Major Powers

The Maldivian Islands are situated in close vicinity of India's south-western tip, about 450 miles away from the Indian mainland. These islands have attracted the interest of old trading powers and of the colonial states of more modern times. But the Maldives were not colonised because of their low resource endowment, hazards of dangerous coral reefs, and an insalubrious climate.

The major colonial powers devised their Indian Ocean strategy until the middle of the 20th century keeping India in view. The traditional colonialism however retreated after the Second World War. The Maldives was never taken over completely by the colonial powers, but the British did develop a 'dependency' relationship with Maldives in 1887 after they subjugated Sri Lanka in 1796.[51] This relationship came to an end only in 1965. Since 1960s with the gradual and eventually complete British withdrawal great power rivalry came into play for the control of the IOR.

In 1941, during World War II, the Royal Navy required an isolated island base with a safe, deep anchorage in a suitably strategic position, and Gan Island met the requirements. The Royal Navy established a base ("Port T") here. This island is located just 240 miles north of the American-base of Diego Garcia. Once available, its facilities were used extensively by the Fleet. The British also had created their airbase at the Gan Island. Gan proved to be of great value during the War, especially after Japanese over-ran Burma and Malaya and started threatening India and Ceylon. This port was a vital link in the convoy route to Australia and for certain operations in the Indian Ocean.

The facilities available at the Gan Island were advertised in the international market after the departure of British.[52] In 1977, the Soviets had approached the Maldives for Gan and offered $ 1 million per year to use it ostensibly as a refuelling and maintenance point for its fishing vessels plying the Indian Ocean. This offer was turned down.[53] The Soviet offer was viewed, as another attempt by them to gain a foothold in the Indian Ocean where the United States, with its base in Diego Garcia, had the dominance. The Soviets succeeded only in signing a cultural and scientific agreement on April 6, 1980, with the Maldives which also created ripples in political circles. After the collapse of the Soviet Union, now another emerging power, China appears keenly interested in the Maldives.

Maldives is fully aware of its critical geo-strategic location. The policy of Maldives so far has been to consciously reduce the effects of foreign influence while making best of a given situation. It has succeeded in eliciting development support from all sides while retaining its independence of actions.

Changing Dynamics of the Indian Ocean Region

The geo-strategic situation of the Indian Ocean Region has dramatically changed with the entry of China. At the same time, the nature of relationship between India and the US has also changed. This has led to change in India's relationship with other important Indian Ocean players like Australia and Japan. However, a Cold War in the IOR is not in the interest of anyone and if the interest of the Chinese is limited only to free flow of energy resources, then China can be integrated into a common approach to energy security in the region. This common approach could focus on security concerns such as dealing with piracy, transnational crime, SAR, maritime safety, and the conduct of joint exercises.

However, it appears that the Chinese interests are limited not only to energy security, they also consider themselves as a major power like the United States, and are quite unwilling to depend on the American protection. They are unwilling to accept the old order and want to create a new order of their own, under their leadership, with their own institutions. Because China doesn't raise questions on political systems, human rights, religious radicalism, and support to terrorism, it is welcomed in many resource-rich countries with dubious political regimes. The Chinese now have the desire to emerge as a maritime power to protect their ever-expanding national interests. This situation however could lead to increased tension in the Indian Ocean region.

The relationship of China with India is quite complex and even ambiguous. This relationship has many positive aspects. For instance, they have flourishing trade and people-to-people relationship. They have also shown convergence on issues like climate change and world trade. But this relationship also has some deep structural problems. The countries have a difficult unresolved border dispute. The trade relationship is also marred by growing imbalance in China's favour. Trade deficit between India and China has increased about 34 per cent to US$ 48.43 billion in 2014-15 from US$ 36.21 billion in the previous fiscal year.[54] China's presence in South Asian countries with whom often India has uneasy relations makes India concerned. China is selling weapons to all India's immediate neighbours, except Bhutan, and its biggest client is Pakistan.[55] It has also constructed deep-water ports in Myanmar, Sri Lanka, and Pakistan. It is also involved in the improvement of Chittagong port in Bangladesh.

The competitive environment prevails in the IOR because of the complexity in the Sino-Indian and Sino-US relations. Besides being complex, these relationships are also multifaceted. China is willing to bide its time with the US as the major world power, but it is less accommodating with smaller regional powers like Australia or even rising powers like India.

Major players of the IOR would like a peaceful rise of China. But it is also feared that their relationship with China might change because of a major diplomatic or strategic crisis, or simply, a series of smaller occurrences. It is feared that China which is basically constructive in its relationship with a still powerful US, may not deal in similar fashion with smaller countries of the region as it rises to power.[56] At present, the geostrategic conditions in the IOR are quite interestingly poised where three main powers—India, China and the US - have their own priorities with potential for conflict.

NOTES

1. Captain A. T. Mahan, *The influence of Sea-Power Upon History 1660-1783*, Natraj Publishers, Dehra Dun, 2003.
2. Robert D. Kaplan, *Monsoon: The Indian Ocean and the Future of American Power*, Random House, New York, 2010.
3. K.M. Panikkar, *India and the Indian Ocean: An Essay on the Influence of Sea Power on Indian History*, Allen & Unwin, London, 1945.
4. Ibid.
5. Geethangani de Silva, "Maritime Issues in South Asia," in Ellen Laipson and Amit Pandya (eds.), *The Indian Ocean: Resource and Governance Challenges*, The Henry L. Stimson Center, Washington, 2009, pp. 43-54.
6. Cdr. P K Ghosh, "Maritime Security Challenges in South Asia and the Indian Ocean: Response Strategies," Paper presented at the Center for Strategic and International Studies, American-Pacific Sealanes Security Institute conference on Maritime Security in Asia, Honolulu, Hawaii, January 18-20, 2004, pp. 2-3.
7. Ibid., p. 7.
8. "17 Nations 15 Ships Demonstrate a Momentous 'Milap': Milan 2014 an Unequivocal Success," Press Information Bureau, Ministry of Defence, Government of India, February 09, 2014, at http://pib.nic.in/newsite/PrintRelease.aspx?relid=103278; also see: Ekatha Ann John, "Milan 2014: Naval Exercise off Andamans Concludes," *The Times of India*, February 10, 2014, at http://timesofindia.indiatimes.com/india/Milan-2014-Naval-exercise-off-Andamans-concludes/articleshow/30149435.cms (Accessed August 15, 2015).
9. Vijay Sakhuja, "Increasing Maritime Competition: IORA, IONS, Milan and the Indian Ocean Networks," Institute of Peace and Conflict Studies, #4320, March 3, 2014, at http://www.ipcs.org/article/india-the-world/increasing-maritime-competition-iora-ions-milan-and-the-indian-ocean-4320.html (Accessed August 16, 2015).
10. Ibid.
11. Cahal Milmo, "Government Told to Renegotiate with US over Use of Diego Garcia for Rendition Flights," *The Independent*, June 19, 2014, at http://www.independent.co.uk/news/uk/politics/government-told-to-renegotiate-with-us-over-use-of-diego-garcia-for-rendition-flights-9546855.html.
12. Richard Norton-Taylor, "David Cameron to Discuss Chagos Islands Sovereignty with Mauritius," *The Guardian*, May 30, 2012, at http://www.theguardian.com/world/2012/may/30/david-cameron-chagos-islands-mauritius.

13. Sandy Gordon, "Strategic Interests of the Major Indian Ocean Powers: An Australian Perspective," in H. Singh (ed.), *Pentagon's South Asia Defence and Strategic Year Book 2010*, Pentagon Press, New Delhi, 2010, at http://ceps.anu.edu.au/publications/pdfs/gordon_strategic_interests_yearbook.pdf
14. John Hendren, "Pentagon Moving B-2 Bombers to New Roosts Closer to Baghdad," *Los Angeles Times*, November 07, 2002, at http://articles.latimes.com/2002/nov/07/world/fg-stealth7 (Accessed August 16, 2015).
15. "India, US Signed Documents to Renew Defence Pact: Agreement Roadmap for Bilateral Defence Ties over the Next Decade," *The Indian Express*, June 4, 2015, at http://indianexpress.com/article/india/india-others/india-us-renew-defence-pact-2/.
16. Jyoti Malhotra, "How India's Pride INS Arihant Was Built," *Business Standard*, August 12, 2013, at http://www.business-standard.com/article/specials/how-india-s-pride-ins-arihant-was-built-113081100745_1.html.
17. "Defining US Indian Ocean Strategy", *The Washington Quarterly*, Spring 2012, Centre for Strategic and International Studies, Washington, pp. 177-178.
18. "Defending Australia in the Asia Pacific Century: Force 2030," Defence White Paper 2009, Department of Defence, Australian Government, p. 96, at http://www.defence.gov.au/CDG/Documents/defence_white_paper_2009.pdf.
19. "CNPC Starts Myanmar-China Oil Pipe Trials to Cut Shipping Time," Bloomberg, January 30, 2015, at http://www.bloomberg.com/news/articles/2015-01-30/cnpc-starts-myanmar-china-oil-pipe-trials-to-cut-shipping-time; also see: "New China-Myanmar Oil Pipeline Bypasses Malacca Trap," *The Hindu*, January 30, 2015, at http://www.thehindu.com/news/international/world/new-chinamyanmar-oil-pipeline-bypasses-malacca-trap/article6839352.ece (Accessed August 16, 2015).
20. Barrister Harun ur Rashid, "Militarisation of the Indian Ocean," *The Daily Star*, April 24, 2010, at http://www.thedailystar.net/pf_story.php?nid=135604.
21. "China's National Defense 2000," November 2000, at http://www.nti.org/db/china/engdocs/wpnd2000.htm.
22. "China's National Defense in 2006," *The Peoples Daily*, at http://english.peopledaily.com.cn/whitepaper/defense2006/defense2006.html; please see the section on National Defense Policy.
23. Tania Branigan, "Chinese Defence Spending to Rise to £56bn," *The Guardian*, March 4, 2011, at http://www.guardian.co.uk/world/2011/mar/04/chinese-defence-spending-rise; also see: "China Defense Budget to Stir Regional Disquiet," Reuters, March 4, 2011, at http://www.reuters.com/article/2011/03/04/us-china-defence-idUSTRE 7230 ZN20110304.
24. China's Defence White Paper, 2015.
25. "Secret Sanya - China's New Nuclear Naval Base Revealed," *IHS Jane's Defense & Security Intelligence & Analysis*, April 21, 2008, at http://www.janes.com/products/janes/defence-security-report.aspx?id=1065927913; also see: "Chinese Nuclear Submarine Base," *The Telegraph*, London, May 1, 2008, at http://www.telegraph.co.uk/news/worldnews/asia/china/1917167/Chinese-nuclear-submarine-base.html.
26. China's Defence White Paper, 2015.
27. "Fresh Reports Circulate on China's Second Aircraft Carrier," Reuters, February 2, 2015, at http://www.reuters.com/article/2015/02/02/us-china-military-idUSKBN0L60K320150202.

28. Harsh V. Pant, "India in the Indian Ocean: Growing Mismatch between Ambitions and Capabilities," *Pacific Affairs*, 82 (2), Summer 2009.
29. Bryan McGrath and Mackenzie Eaglen, "Why China Wants Aircraft Carriers," *The National Interest*, June 9, 2015, at http://nationalinterest.org/feature/why-china-wants-aircraft-carriers-13071.
30. Sachin Parashar, "Chinese Submarine Docking in Lanka 'Inimical' to India's Interests: Govt," *The Times of India*, November 3, 2014, at http://timesofindia.indiatimes.com/india/Chinese-submarine-docking-in-Lanka-inimical-to-Indias-interests-Govt/articleshow/45025487.cms.
31. Saibal Dasgupta, "China Defends Docking of Its Submarine in Sri Lanka," *The Times of India*, November 4, 2014,at http://timesofindia.indiatimes.com/india/China-defends-docking-of-its-submarine-in-Sri-Lanka/articleshow/45029781.cms.
32. "NZ Navy Chief on Chinese Foray in Indian Ocean," PTI, June 17, 2015, at http://timesofindia.indiatimes.com/india/NZ-navy-chief-on-Chinese-foray-in-Indian-Ocean/articleshow/47709082.cms.
33. Sachin Parashar, "China in South China Sea and Indian Ocean: A quest for pre-eminence in Asia," *The Times of India*, May 24, 2015, at http://timesofindia.indiatimes.com/world/china/China-in-South-China-Sea-and-Indian-Ocean-A-quest-for-pre-eminence-in-Asia/articleshow/47406036.cms.
34. Ibid.
35. Author's interview with J. J. Robinson, Editor, *Minivan News*, Malé.
36. Based on an interview conducted in Sri Lanka; identity not disclosed on request.
37. D.S. Rajan, "China in the Indian Ocean: Competing Priorities," IPCS, #4302, February 10, 2014, at http://www.ipcs.org/article/india/china-in-the-indian-ocean-competing-priorities-4302.html.
38. Wang Jisi, "March West: China's Geopolitical Strategy of Rebalancing," *Global Times*, October 17, 2012.
39. Yun Sun, "March West: China's Response to the U.S. Rebalancing," Brookings, January 31, 2013, at http://www.brookings.edu/blogs/up-front/posts/2013/01/31-china-us-sun.
40. Teshu Singh, "China & Southeast Asia: What is the Strategy behind the Maritime Silk Road," IPCS, #4142, October 15, 2013, at http://www.ipcs.org/article/china/china-and-asean-revisiting-the-maritime-silk-road-4142.html.
41. Vijay Sakhuja, "The Maritime Silk Route and the Chinese Charm Offensive," IPCS, #4310, February 17, 2014, at http://www.ipcs.org/article/china/the-maritime-silk-route-and-the-chinese-charm-offensive-4310.html.
42. Dilip Hiro, "Beijing's Maritime Silk Road Passes through Islamabad: With Strong Ties to Pakistan, China Extends Economic and Strategic Influence over the Indian Ocean Region," *YaleGlobal*, July 21, 2015, at http://yaleglobal.yale.edu/content/beijing%E2%80%99s-maritime-silk-road-passes-through-islamabad (Accessed August 17, 2015).
43. Saibal Dasgupta, "Chinese Submarine Dives into Indian Ocean to Hunt for Gold," *The Times of India*, January 5, 2015, at http://timesofindia.indiatimes.com/india/Chinese-submarine-dives-into-Indian-Ocean-to-hunt-for-gold/articleshow/45754934.cms.
44. Vijay Sakhuja, "China in the Indian Ocean: Deep Sea Forays," IPCS, #4286, February

3, 2014, at http://www.ipcs.org/article/china/china-in-the-indian-ocean-deep-sea-forays-4286.html.

45. "China Proposes Joint Mining of Indian Ocean with India," *The Times of India*, May 7, 2015, at http://timesofindia.indiatimes.com/india/China-proposes-joint-mining-of-Indian-Ocean-with-India/articleshow/47184739.cms.
46. Vijay Sakhuja, No. 46.
47. "NSA Level Meeting on trilateral Maritime Security Cooperation between India, Sri Lanka and Maldives," Ministry of External Affairs, Government of India, March 06, 2014, at http://mea.gov.in/in-focus-article.htm?23037/NSA+level+meeting+on+trilateral+Maritime+Security+Cooperation+between+India+Sri+Lanka+and+Maldives.
48. R.K. Radhakrishnan, "India, Sri Lanka, Maldives to Sign Agreement on Maritime Cooperation," *The Hindu*, December 15, 2012.
49. Iranga Kahangama, "India, Sri Lanka and Maldives: Tripartite Maritime Security Agreement and Growing Chinese Influence," IPCS, #4058, July 30, 2013, at http://www.ipcs.org/article/india/ipcs-debate-india-sri-lanka-and-maldives-the-tripartite-maritime-4058.html (Accessed August 17, 2015).
50. C. Raja Mohan, "Modi And The Indian Ocean: Restoring India's Sphere Of Influence," Asia Maritime Transparency Initiative, June 18, 2015, at http://amti.csis.org/modi-and-the-indian-ocean-restoring-indias-sphere-of-influence/
51. Urmila Phadnis and Ela Dutt Luithui, "The Maldives Enter World Politics," *Asian Affairs*, 8(3), January-February 1981, pp. 167.
52. Ibid.
53. Ibid.
54. "India-China trade deficit swells 34% to $48 billion," *The Hindu*, May 13, 2015, at http://www.thehindu.com/news/national/indiachina-trade-deficit-swells-34-to-48-billion/article7201545.ece.
55. Charles Clover, "Chinese Arms Sales Surge 143% in 5 Years," *Financial Times*, London, March 16, 2015, at http://www.ft.com/cms/s/0/52eb31a4-cb99-11e4-aeb5-00144feab7de.html#axzz3ixI7zreE.
56. "China: Working with US on 'Great Power Relations'," China Central Television, June 19, 2015, at http://english.cntv.cn/2015/06/19/VIDE1434718560966593.shtml; also see: Cheng Li and Lucy Xu, "Chinese Enthusiasm and American Cynicism Over the 'New Type of Great Power Relations'," The Brookings Institution, December 4, 2014, at http://www.brookings.edu/research/opinions/2014/12/05-chinese-pessimism-american-cynicism-great-power-li-xu (Accessed August 16, 2015).

8

Maldives and the Great Game in the Indian Ocean Region

The Indian Ocean has always been at the centre stage of the global geo-politics. The Maldives lies at the central point of all key sea routes in the IOR. For this reason, the Maldives has also been a centre of attraction for global powers. The post-Cold War era saw eclipse of the Soviet Union but also a progressive rise of China, which now seems to be a claimant for the space vacated by the former communist giant. China has already suggested a dialogue for a great power relationship with the US. This, in other words, means China considers itself as another global power like the US. China under its incumbent President Xi Jinping wants to be a maritime power. It is no longer satisfied with the protection of its shores. To achieve this objective, China has suggested revival of the Silk Route, which, as mentioned earlier, has both overland and maritime components. Actually, the MSR is far bigger than the overland component.

To defend its overseas interests, China now wants to build a blue water navy. It has successfully roped in both Sri Lanka and the Maldives for its MSR project. What is more important, the Chinese are now sending ships and submarines in the Indian Ocean that has turned them into an important player in this region. Thus, like other great powers of the past, China has also intensified its economic and military activities in the Indian

Ocean. It has succeeded in getting a major presence in both the Maldives and Sri Lanka, the two important island nations which are located very close to India. Besides China, the only remaining superpower of the world, the United States, also remains interested in the Maldives. Other powers like Japan and Saudi Arabia too are interested. This situation has created considerable difficulty for Indian foreign policy in this region.

Recently, there has been a re-orientation in the Maldivian foreign policy, wherein the Chinese enjoy a place of much greater influence than they did in the past. On the other hand, the earlier bonhomie between India and the Maldives has been reduced. This has implications for Indian security and strategic interests. Even the Western powers including the US are finding it difficult to deal with the Maldives. To counter their pressure, the Maldives has tried to use both Saudi Arabia and China. However, what makes the whole strategic scenario further interesting is the friendly overture of the Maldives to Japan. Thus, barring Russians, who were busy in Crimea, the Maldivians seem to be handling all the major powers of the world – making Indian Ocean the hub of global geo-politics.

Maldives and Chinese Strategic Considerations

After the British quit the Maldives in 1976 and the Soviet Union disintegrated in the early 1990s, China emerged as a major power in the world. This China is different from the China fifty years ago and has a growing economy based on exports, which are dependent on energy and raw material imports. To sustain this growth pace, it is necessary that the SLOCs are kept open. In recent times, the SLOCs in the IOR have been threatened by non-conventional security threats like piracy, in the Gulf of Aden, for example. So far, this has been guaranteed by the US. But China is aware that its relentless growth will lead to friction with the only remaining superpower. Already this tension is evident in many areas. Hence, China, which clearly does not want to depend on the US to keep its trade and commerce going, is gradually working towards fulfilling its core strategic interests in the IOR.

The foremost interest of China in the Indian Ocean is to protect its increasingly important supplies of energy, raw materials, and finished goods that need to transit the IOR. Most importantly, China now sees itself as a long-term competitor of the US. It also expects resistance from India, a major regional power to its power projection in the Indian Ocean. Besides, in last 200 years it has been the mark of a great power to have bases abroad. It was so in the case of Great Britain, the US and the former Soviet Union. China is also keen to acquire bases, because it senses that its emergence as great power is only a matter of time.

These strategic considerations have been reflected in China's military planning. Initially, an attempt was made to describe Chinese strategic planning as the encirclement of India by a 'string of pearls'. The term, string of pearls, was coined in 2003 by a team of Booz Allen consultants, in a report for the Pentagon, to describe China's attempts to gain a strategic foothold in the Indian Ocean.[1] Soon, string of pearls came to mean encirclement of India by China. However, it would not be proper to describe China's military planning as a 'string of pearls' strategy for India, rather it reflects its global military aspirations.[2]

Chinese Quest for Military Bases

The issue of overseas military and naval bases has been debated hotly in China since the country joined the international anti-piracy cooperation in 2009 off the coast of Somalia. Generally, the Chinese military has been secretive about its intentions, but in recent times, some of its strategists are far more assertive. The Chinese strategists like Shen Dingli now openly talk about the need to have bases for the Chinese Navy and military.

Shen Dingli argues that current Chinese overseas interests demand setting up of military bases.[3] He thinks that the Chinese Navy is now going to play a crucial role in safeguarding the core interests of the country. He does not consider terrorism as a serious threat but is more concerned about the piracy off the coast of Somalia and in the Gulf of Aden. He also takes secessionism outside Chinese mainland (Taiwan) far more seriously. To meet these challenges, he advocates that China should set up its own blue water navy and should rely on overseas military bases to cut the supply costs. He expects that in future China may also be in great demand for military protection. He suggests that there is no need to call these military bases as such. What is important is that they should allow Chinese ships to harbour and provide facilities for its naval personnel to take rest. He thinks that the host countries would welcome such military bases if they are in their interests and can maintain regional stability.[4] Further, Shen Dingli is, obviously, aware that Chinese attempts to establish military bases abroad is going to face resistance from big powers like the US, France, and Britain who already have their military bases abroad, but he exhorts China not to be deterred by this.

Moreover, *Global Times,* the nationalist Chinese newspaper, too, has argued for the establishment of overseas military bases. In an opinion column, it said, "However, if China is going to play an important role in the Asia-Pacific region and on the international stage, as urged by the international community, it eventually will need to establish overseas military bases in cooperation with other countries."[5]

It is quite obvious that protecting China's overseas interests has now almost become its core national interest, which is now no less significant than its 'One China policy'. This objective puts the focus on to the Indian Ocean, where the Maldives enjoys a strategically critical position. Therefore, it is hardly surprising that China has been trying to woo the Maldives so that it also follows a policy similar to many of India's neighbours who have voluntarily given space to China with the hope to balance India and also to benefit from its growing economic muscle.

China has been trying for naval bases or facilities much before this debate about naval bases reached a conclusion in the country. Intense diplomatic activities were witnessed between China and the Maldives towards the closing years of the 20th century. This was the period when both India and China were trying to woo the Maldives for its strategic importance.[6]

In July 2001 some reports indicated that China had managed to coax the Maumoon Abdul Gayoom government to allow it to establish a base on one of its islands close to the capital, Malé.[7] In this endeavour, the Pakistanis had supposedly helped the Chinese. It was also suggested that after two years of negotiation the deal was finalised on May 17, 2001 when the Chinese Prime Minister, Zhu Rongji, had visited Malé to inaugurate a China-funded housing project. These reports were however completely speculative, and the Chinese still don't have a military or naval base in the Maldives.[8]

In 2011, when Nasheed was in power, some Maldivian policymakers argued that it was difficult for China to get a base in the Maldives because of a constitutional ban on foreign powers getting bases in the country. They felt that Maldivian politicians often raise the possibility of China getting a base in the Maldives to keep India concerned.[9] They asserted that the primary security collaboration of the Maldives was with India. While it is true that for its security during the Nasheed era, the Maldives primarily collaborated with India, the constitution however did not bar foreign powers from having bases in that country.[10] It was possible to get this facility on a lease of 99 years.

After the assumption of power by Nasheed, the Chinese influence in the Maldives did come down, but they kept trying to bag crucial development projects. They were particularly interested in developing Ihavandhoo and Maarandhoo Islands, with transhipment ports, among other things. They also showed an interest in the development of the country's second international airport at Hanimaadhoo. These islands are located in the Haa Alif Atoll, situated in the north of Maldives.[11] The main objective behind Chinese interest in these projects was to get a foothold in the Indian Ocean.

During Nasheed's period, the policymakers of the Maldives believed that the Indian Ocean should be for the Indian Ocean People.[12] In case China was interested in the Maldives, then it should use the normal ports and should not think of constructing new ones. There was a perception that the Maldivians themselves would not allow giving any land for military base in the Maldives and this foreign policy was difficult to sustain.[13] Maldivians during this period were holding military exercises with the US and Indian military. They wanted to continue a balanced foreign policy which was pursued even during the Cold War era.[14]

The Chinese influence over the Maldives increased when Waheed came to power and has remained so even under the present government of Abdulla Yameen. In May 2014, some reports speculated that India and China were competing with each other to construct a naval base in one of Maldives' atolls to berth its coastguard ships. This project was estimated to be worth Rs. 3,000 crore and could have also boosted Maldivian flourishing tourism sector with a docking facility for commercial ships.[15] However, subsequently, the Defence Minister, Mohamed Nazim, denied receiving any "official" proposals from India to develop a dockyard in the Maldives, saying that the project would not be handed over to a foreign army.[16]

Maldives Amends Constitution to Enable Foreign Ownership of Land

In a move seen largely to forge closer ties with China, the Maldives amended its constitution on July 22, 2015, which will allow foreign ownership of land. The unicameral parliament of the Maldives passed a bill that amended Article 251 of the Constitution. The amendment was proposed by the Abdulla Yameen-led PPM government and was passed with 70 votes in favour and 14 against, with one MP absent. This constitutional amendment bill has added a new chapter to the Maldives Constitution. It was ratified by President Yameen the very next day.

The original Article 251 of the Constitution had prohibited foreign ownership of land. It said that:

(a) No foreign party, shall own or be given ownership of any part of the territory of the Maldives.
(b) A foreign party shall not receive a lease of, or be given in any other way, any part of the territory of the Maldives for a period exceeding 99 years.
(c) No part of the territory of the Maldives shall be used for foreign military purposes without the approval of the majority of the total membership of the People's Majlis.

The constitutional amendment however changes this situation. Now foreigners are allowed to own freehold land in the Maldives as long as they meet certain criteria, including that the project built on the land must be approved by Parliament, there must be a minimum investment of US$ 1 billion "in the territory of the Maldives", and upon the project's reaching completion, "at least 70 per cent of the land must have been reclaimed from the ocean and be visible at medium tide". It also declares that allowing a foreign party to own land under these specific circumstances "does not undermine the Maldivian state's sovereignty over its territory and does not amount to loss of territory".

The constitutional amendment has caused controversy both inside the country as well as outside. The Maldivian Government defends this step and says that the new law is meant to attract mega development projects and create employment in the country. On the contrary, the opposition says that the amendment is intended to facilitate the extension of China's influence and foothold in the IOR. It will enable Chinese investment in the Maldives, and could possibly pave the way for Chinese military facilities in the country. The opposition also questioned the speed with which this amendment was passed without adequate consultation and parliamentary debate.

This constitutional amendment has caused concern in India, which is geographically closest to the Maldives, and also among other nations whose vital economic and strategic interests are linked to the Indian Ocean. Theoretically, it is true that Indian investors too can buy land, provided they are willing to invest $ 1 billion and reclaim land, the road looks difficult for them as of now. Moreover, the conditions laid down are such that they suit China which has been reclaiming land from the sea in recent times especially in the South China Sea. With growing Chinese interest in the Indian Ocean, it is only expected that Beijing would try to further expand its footprint in the region.

To express Indian concern, the Foreign Secretary, S Jaishankar, visited the Maldives and discussed the issue with its top political leadership. He also handed over a letter of Indian Prime Minister Modi expressing concern. It was one of the rarest cases where the top political leadership of India expressed concern.[17] The Maldivian President, Abdulla Yameen, however tried to assure the Indian Government in a letter sent to the Indian Foreign Minister that the Indian Ocean would remain "a demilitarised zone".[18]

Interestingly, the Chinese Foreign Ministry has also claimed that it is not planning to build military bases on the Maldives and considers constitutional amendment its internal matter.[19] At the same time, it has also stated that its firms may take up land for commercial use.[20] The Chinese are however known to use civilian facilities for military purposes.

Chinese state-run firms can use such facilities as listening posts and as sites for military radars tracking Indian ships and planes. This development is in line with the shift in foreign policy of the President Abdulla Yameen's government who has been trying to come closer to China.

Chinese Military Diplomacy with the Maldives

China has been quite keen to establish a relationship with the Maldivian military. The Chinese are aware that a military or naval base in the Maldives would put them firmly in control of the oil route stretching from the Strait of Malacca to the Strait of Hormuz. It will also increase their dominance over the sea lanes.

However, any permanent Chinese military presence in the Maldives is not liked by either India or the US. The Maldives is a soft underbelly of both Indian and American security. To counter Chinese military diplomacy with the Maldives, the US had sent its Navy Chief, Dennis Blair, to the Maldives a month after Rongji's May 2001 visit. The US has a military base in Diego Garcia and any Chinese naval base in the Maldives would allow the Chinese to monitor the US military activities in the region.

In July 2001, China had planned to conduct joint marine and deep-sea patrolling exercises with the Maldives but it backed off. China claimed that the exercises were sought by the Maldives, but the Maldives maintained a silence over the issue. The exercises while innocuous were typical of the Chinese strategy of creeping expansionism. The Chinese however backed off because they did not want to provoke the US at that point in time.

The Chinese at the time were facing threat of the US sanctions for supplying M-9 and M-11 missiles to Pakistan. Moreover, the World Trade Organisation (WTO) meeting was coming up in Doha and China did not want the US to block its entry into the WTO for any reason. Finally, the incident of the Chinese forced landing of a US navy spy plane in April 2001 had already angered the US military.[21] Weighing all the pros and cons the Chinese decided that it was not judicious to provoke the US.

The first official contact between the Chinese and Maldives' armies started in September 2002 when the Maldivian State Minister for Defence and National Security paid a friendly visit to China at the invitation of the Central Military Commission. Though the visit of Maldivian military officials had taken place in the past, they were not at the invitation of the Chinese military.

During Nasheed's tenure, there was an attempt to sign a defence agreement with the Chinese. But this plan became known and the Maldives promised not to do this again. In this period there were no defence relations between China and the Maldives. India and the US remained two main defence and strategic partners of the Maldives, and the Maldivian security forces were trained by them. Chinese, however, continued to lobby in the Maldives.[22]

When Waheed was in power, both he and his defence minister visited China and signed agreements. Under the present regime of Abdulla Yameen, no major defence agreement has been signed. However, 20 Maldivian police officers attended a China-Maldives Police Service Seminar along with their Chinese counterparts in Shanghai held from April 10-23, 2014. The Maldivian Police Commissioner, Hussain Waheed, believed that the participation of Maldivian police officers in the seminar would improve their standards and bring them at par with the Chinese officers. Even when Chinese President Xi Jinping visited the Maldives in 2014, defence issues were carefully avoided keeping the sensitivity of India.

Negotiation of the US-Maldives SOFA Agreement

In the IOR, the United States remains the strongest power because of its military base at Diego-Garcia. In recent times, it has tried to further strengthen its position. It is also aware of the Chinese ambition to project power in the Indian Ocean and its desire to use the Maldives as a tool for this objective. No wonder, Americans have attempted to take the Maldives in their own fold and one way of doing it has been to persuade the Maldives to sign a SOFA with it.

Though the diplomatic relationship between the United States and the Maldives was established in 1966 after the archipelago nation got its freedom from Britain in 1965, the United States still has no consular or diplomatic offices in the Maldives. Its Ambassador and many embassy staff in Sri Lanka are accredited to the Maldives and make periodic visits. However, for a long time, the American Embassy in Sri Lanka which is supposed to look after Maldives remained focused on the civil war taking place in Sri Lanka and did not place even a diplomat to the Maldives. The Maldives too has no embassy in Washington, DC, and its permanent representative to the UN in New York is accredited as ambassador to the United States.

The United States has been aware of the importance of promoting security in the Indian Ocean. Despite this, Maldives was not seriously on the American radar until 9/11 when it had to deal with Ibrahim Fauzi, a Maldivian national. Fauzi was one of the terror suspects captured in Pakistan and detained in Guantanamo Bay. Americans appeared not even quite familiar with Gayoom and the system of administration that he followed in his country.

However, in recent years, there has been a sudden increase in the strategic importance of the Maldives for the Americans. This has been particularly so after the US announced its pivot to Asia policy, but was refused military bases by Bangladesh, Sri Lanka, and India, and its relationship with Pakistan also became uncertain.

The US is now trying to establish a close military-to-military relationship with the Maldives. This includes joint exercises and training opportunities for Maldivian officers at the US service academies. The US naval vessels have regularly called at the Maldives in recent years. The US military got access to some Maldivian infrastructure following a number of agreements in the 2000s. In 2001-2002, the Maldives extended strong support to the US efforts to combat terrorism and terrorist financing. In 2010, Washington signed an Acquisition and Cross Service Agreement (ACSA) with the previous government of President Mohamed Nasheed.[23] This agreement allows the US to use its airport and sea port facilities.

The US claims to promote democratic reform in the Maldives and when Gayoom was in power it urged him to maintain the timeline that was set out in the government's March 2006 "Reform Roadmap". The US called on all Maldivian parties to chart a way forward respecting Maldivian democratic institutions, the rule of law, and the will of the Maldivian people following the February 2012 transfer of power in the Maldives. However, this US commitment to democracy in the Maldives came under close scrutiny when Waheed was in power and the democratic movement in the Maldives believed that he had assumed power in a coup d'état.

In the rebellion against Mohamed Nasheed, Mohamed Nazim, who subsequently became defence minister during the regime of Waheed and later under Abdualla Yameen, was seen as one of the coup leaders by the pro-democracy movement in the Maldives. Interestingly, Nazim, was believed to be quite close to Michele Sison, then US ambassador (to Sri Lanka and the Maldives). It appears that the US recognised Waheed's regime because in the changeover, Nazim had played a key role and under the new dispensation the US was expecting considerable benefits.

The US also tried to legitimise the Waheed regime and the transfer of power before they signed various agreements with Waheed's government. It was done with the help of Commission of National Inquiry (CoNI) report and with the support of the UN secretary General, Ban Ki Moon, who lost no time endorsing the CONI report.[24] This was an example of the US giving up its stated principles as it tried to negotiate with a regime that came to power in a violent, illegal coup.

The Americans signed as agreement with the Defence Minister, Mohamed Nazim, to establish a Maritime Surveillance System in order to monitor and identify vessels operating inside the Maldivian territorial waters. It has been established in seven strategic locations including Villi-Malé, Haa Alif Atoll Uligan, Kaafu Atoll Maafilaafushi, Laamu Atoll Kahdhoo, Gaaf Alif Atoll Kaadehdhoo, Seenu Atoll Gan, and Gnaviyani Atoll Fuvahmulah. The system is supposed to enable military to identify and provide enhanced situational awareness of the vessels inside Maldivian waters. It will also give the MNDF the ability to contact and send messages to the vessels. Nazim hailed the system as a major boost to the national security of the Maldives and said it would also benefit neighbouring countries in the Indian Ocean. He ritualistically also mentioned the importance of maintaining close ties with neighbouring India and Sri Lanka in order to protect Maldivian waters.

Moreover, the Defence Minister, Mohamed Nazim, and the US Ambassador to Sri Lanka and the Maldives, Michele J Sison, signed an MoU to provide it with a border control system. The Maldives had decided not to use the border control system provided by Malaysia-based IT group

Nexbis because of the charges of corruption in getting the contract. Afterwards, to fill the void the Indian High Commissioner, Dnyaneshwar Mulay, handed over a new Advance Passenger Information System (APIS) to immigration authorities at the Ibrahim Nasir International Airport (INIA) that was designed to provide passport information and other details of incoming travellers before their arrival.

Despite this, Nazim entered into an agreement with the Americans and said that the system proposed under the MoU would be provided free of charge to the Maldives and would save the country Mf 500 million (US$ 35 million). However, former Immigration Controller and then State Defence Minister, Ilyas Hussain Ibrahim, expressed concern that the US involvement in the border control system would allow the country to exert its influence on Maldivian affairs. He thought that this would allow the US to take control of the system and use it to locate foreign nationals whenever it wished. It effectively put the US in control of entry points into the island from the outside world.

The US also engaged the Maldivian regime in a joint military training exercise centred around Gan from October 6-17, 2012. It appears that after announcing its rebalancing policy towards Asia, Americans have been eying the Gan base of the Maldives. Gan was originally built by Britain and served as a key operational base during the World War II. Britain with great reluctance handed it over to the Maldives only in 1976. Britain still regrets vacating this base and since then Americans have been trying to regain it.

Clearly, Americans tried to closely engage with the Waheed regime. The Indian media, on the other hand, unleashed a campaign which presented a picture of imminent takeover of the Maldives by elements aligned to Al Qaeda. This kind of campaign suited the US and could have been used as an excuse to intervene in the Maldives. During this period the Maldives saw repeated visits by the US Assistant Secretary, Robert Blake. Interestingly, after Blake's visit in September 2012 the international community decided to ease pressure on the Maldivian authorities to return to the democratic path and the rule of law.[25] It appears that both Washington and London were acting in tandem. While Indians were working on a containment strategy, Americans on the contrary were trying to engage the regime more closely.

The US intentions in the Maldives became public when its negotiation with the Maldives on the SOFA was leaked to the media. The US embassy conceded that such talks were going on and they had consulted even India on it, but denied any plans for a permanent American base.[26] It said, "SOFAs are normal practice wherever the Unites States cooperates closely with a country's national security forces and they generally establish the framework under which US personnel operate in a country when supporting security-related activities and the United States is currently party to more than 100 agreements that may be considered a SOFA."

The Maldivian Defence Minister, Mohamed Nazim, also refuted rumours suggesting that the United States had proposed to establish a military base in the Maldives. However, he did agree that the SOFA proposal was being discussed with the relevant authorities of the Maldives and would be signed on the advice of the Attorney General. He also claimed that the Maldivian Government would not allow any foreign government to establish a military base in the country. He even argued that such a cross-service agreement was signed during former President Mohamed Nasheed's government and it was not a new proposal.

Just a month before (in March 2013) a top-level delegation from the Maldives was invited to visit a US Aircraft Carrier, USS John C Stennis, at sea, as it passed by the Maldives. The Maldivian delegation included the Vice President, Mohamed Waheed Deen; Defence Minister, Mohamed Nazim; Home Minister, Dr Mohamed Jameel Ahmed; Tourism Minister, Ahmed Adeeb; Police Commissioner, Abdulla Riyaz; and some top officers of the MNDF. The other participants were the US Ambassador to the Maldives and Sri Lanka, Michele J Sison; Defense Attache, LTC Patrick J Schuler; and Indian Defence Advisor to the Maldives and First Secretary of the Indian High Commission in Malé, P S Karthigeyan.[27]

Though both the US and Maldives tried to present SOFA as a benign document, its implications appeared far more serious and sweeping. The draft agreement incorporated "the principal provisions and necessary authorisations for the temporary presence and activities of United States forces in the Republic of Maldives and, in the specific situations indicated herein, the presence and activities of United States contractors in the Republic of Maldives".

The draft SOFA also authorised the "United States forces to exercise all rights and authorities with Agreed Facilities and Areas that are necessary for their use, operation, defence or control, including the right to undertake new construction works and make alterations and improvements". Moreover, it envisaged that the Maldives would "furnish, without charge" to the US unspecified "Agreed Facilities and Areas", and "such other facilities and areas in the territory and territorial seas of the Republic of Maldives as may be provided by the Republic of Maldives in the future". It specified: "The Republic of the Maldives authorizes United States forces to exercise all rights and authorities with Agreed Facilities and Areas that are necessary for their use, operation, defence or control, including the right to undertake new construction works and make alterations and improvements." It further authorised the US to "control entry" to areas provided for its "exclusive use", and permitted it to operate its own telecommunications system and use the radio spectrum "free of cost to the United States".

Besides, the US would also be granted access to and use of "aerial ports, sea ports and agreed facilities for transit, support and related activities; bunkering of ships, refuelling of aircraft, maintenance of vessels, aircraft, vehicles and equipment, accommodation of personnel, communications, ship visits, training, exercises, humanitarian activities".

Interestingly, the SOFA conferred on the US personnel (and civilian staff) "the privileges, exemptions and immunities equivalent to those accorded to the administrative and technical staff of a diplomatic mission under the Vienna Convention", and guaranteed that the Maldives laws won't be applicable to the US personnel, who will be subject exclusively to the criminal jurisdiction of the United States.

The US personnel and contractors would also be permitted to import and export personal property, equipment, supplies and technology without licence, restriction or inspection, or the payment of any taxes, charges or customs duties. Most important, the vessels and vehicles operated by, and for, US forces would be permitted to enter and move freely within the territorial seas of the Maldives, free from boarding, inspection or the payment of landing, parking, port or harbour fees.

Clearly, the SOFA proposed by the Americans would have resulted in their military presence in the Maldives and that would have brought a tectonic shift in the geopolitics of the IOR.

India Striving to Maintain Security Environment of Indian Ocean

The security environment in the Indian Ocean is facing pulls and pressure from a number of territorial and extra-territorial players. The Maldives is now more open to international engagements. That could be because of increased globalisation that is taking place the world over. In the Maldives during Nasheed's period the UK and US were considered major diplomatic partners whereas India was considered its major security partner.

The defence cooperation between India and the Maldives ranges from training and joint combat exercises to help in maritime surveillance and supply of military equipment to the archipelago. The Coast Guards of two countries have been conducting joint training exercises codenamed "DOSTI" since 1991 in addition to other joint defense interactions.[28] Subsequently, these exercises were expanded to include Sri Lanka in 2012, thus making it a trilateral exercise. The aim of these exercises is to further fortify the friendship, enhance mutual operational capability, and exercise interoperability and to build cooperation between the Coast Guards of Maldives, India and Sri Lanka. The "DOSTI-XII" joint exercises were conducted by the Indian Coast Guard with the Maldives National Defence Force (MNDF) and the Sri Lankan Coast Guard at Malé, Maldives from 28-31 October 2014. The focus of these exercises was on Maritime Search and Rescue (M-SAR), Humanitarian Assistance and Disaster Relief (HADR), Marine Pollution Response (POLRES) and Anti-piracy operations. For the first time the exercise were also be viewed by representatives from maritime forces of Seychelles and Mauritius.

India and the Maldives also have a joint Military Training Exercise codenamed "EKUVERIN". This bilateral annual exercise commenced in 2009 at Belgaum, India. It is held annually, alternately in India and Maldives with the aim of enhancing military cooperation and interoperability between defence forces of the two countries. The sixth joint Military Training Exercise between the Indian Army and the Maldives National Defence Force (MNDF) was held at Thiruvananthapuram in

2015. In this joint exercise, forty five marines from the Maldivian National Defence Force and a same number of Indian infantry troops participated.[29]

When the Indian Defence Minister, A K Anthony, visited the Maldives in August 2009, he signed a defence cooperation agreement with the Maldives. As per that agreement, the Indian Navy and the MNDF would carry out joint surveillance and patrolling activities in the Indian Ocean. New Delhi agreed to provide a Dhruv helicopter and help establish a 25-bed military hospital in the island chain.[30] It was also reported that India would establish a network of ground radars in all its 26 atolls in the country and link them up with the Indian coastal command.[31] A section in the Maldives had tried to oppose the agreement stating that "Maldivian sovereignty was under threat and that the country was becoming an Indian protectorate".[32] The Maldives however continues to accord great importance to security cooperation with India, as its vital tourist industry depended (and still depends) on security in the IOR. India helps the Maldives by regularly patrolling its territorial waters with both warships and reconnaissance aircraft.

Things however changed in the area of defence cooperation with the exit of Nasheed. Waheed signed a defence cooperation agreement with China. Yameen too initially appeared closer to China. The internal power struggle in the Maldives had caused a chill in its relationship with India. This relationship has now once again started improving with some quiet diplomacy. When India's External Affairs Minister Sushma Swaraj visited Maldives in October 2015, she emphasised the Government of India policy of 'Neighbours First' in her meeting with President Yameen. Interestingly, President Yameen also reiterated Maldives' policy of 'India First'.

Sushma Swaraj was in the Maldives in October 2015 to co-chair the 5th Meeting of the India-Maldives Joint Commission. The Joint Commission was set up under the 1986 Agreement on Economic and Technical Cooperation and first met in Malé in 1990. The Framework Agreement for Cooperation, signed in November 2011, mandated the Joint Commission to broaden its cross sectoral emphasis to include defense and security related issues.

Thus for the first time defence and security relationship was discussed in the Joint Commission meeting. The Maldivian side acknowledged the usefulness of the Advanced Light Helicopter given by India in the development of aviation capacities in the Maldives. The Ministers were of the view that the bilateral partnership was important also for maintaining security in the Indian Ocean Region. It was felt that increased cooperation would help in meeting the common threat from radicalism and terrorism and combat the growing menace of drug trafficking and financing of terrorism in the region.

India and the Maldives also have initiated active counter-terrorism mechanisms to thwart any future seaborne terror attacks on the Indian soil, similar to the 26/11 attacks in Mumbai. This joint counter-terrorism mechanism will include active intelligence sharing on a continual basis aimed at specifically nullifying any sort of misadventure that may be attempted by terrorist organisations such as Al-Qaeda, Islamic State of Iraq and Syria (ISIS).

India now seems to have adopted a two-pronged strategy to maintain a favourable maritime environment in the IOR. It is now willing to adopt a robust maritime diplomacy to effectively counter the ever-expanding Chinese strategic footprint in the entire IOR. With this objective India dispatched its largest and most potent warship, aircraft carrier INS Vikramaditya, accompanied by destroyer INS Mysore and tanker INS Deepak, to Maldives in February 2016.[33] Before that the INS Vikramaditya had made its first-ever foreign port call at Colombo on 21-22January 2016. These port calls reaffirmed India's abiding commitment to be "the net security provider" in the IOR.

India is however also willing to cooperate with other littorals to provide security to the 'Global Commons.'[34] This was the main objective of the International Fleet Review held in Visakhapatnam in February 2016. The participation in the fleet review this time had gone to nearly 50 whereas only 21 navies had participated in 2001 when the event was last held. As many as 24 foreign warships, including two each from the US and China, were anchored off Visakhapatnam, apart from the 71-odd vessels from India.

India thinks that the ever-growing importance of the Indian Ocean Region and the existing threats to maritime interests means that the stake holder coastal countries would have to sit together and discuss possible partnerships for a secure future. Even in the 21st century, threats from piracy loom large and there are issues like asymmetric warfare and maritime terrorism. No country can tackle these threats by itself. These challenges would have to be dealt with in cooperation with other countries.

The Emerging Security Scenario in the IOR

The security scenario in the IOR has fundamentally changed with the emergence of China as a major power on the global scene. In the past, the players participating in the rivalry for control over the IOR region were limited. In the 19th and 20th centuries, Britain was the predominant naval power in this region. Subsequently, this position was taken over by the US with its base in Diego-Garcia. Though the former Soviet Union tried, it could never challenge the supremacy of the US in the IOR.

In the present times, however, this security scenario has considerably changed. It has actually become quite complex and this complexity is very well reflected in the Maldivian foreign policy towards various countries who have interests in this region. Though the US still remains the only superpower in the world, there is considerable decline in its position. Some even go to the extent of suggesting that the world has already become multi-polar. Though the US remains a major pole, China, Russia, India, and a few others constitute other poles. Besides the US, among the other poles, the rise of China has been quite dramatic, so much so that China now sees itself almost equal to the US in status.

China's rise in the economic and military power has allowed it to enter the IOR in a major way, and it is trying to strengthen its foothold. The Maldives figures prominently in China's desire to achieve this objective. The Chinese are using their chequebook diplomacy and their ability to deliver on infrastructural projects to woo countries like the Maldives and Sri Lanka. Their attraction has been so great that the Maldivians could not ignore China even when an India-friendly democratic regime of President Nasheed was in power. The Chinese attraction for Maldivians has grown after Waheed came to power and has continued to remain so under the present regime of Abdulla Yameen.

China is expanding its economic diplomacy globally. The Maldives is no exception. China has been successful in making inroads into the

Maldivian economy and polity. However, Nasheed exercised some caution in developing the relationship with China and did not want to disturb his favourable equation with India. During his period, the administration in Malé viewed Indian and Maldivian security as interdependent and the bilateral relations of the two countries were robust. India remained a key player in the Maldives' security dynamics.[35]

China, on the other hand, has been pursuing a strategy that would enable it to establish a base in the Maldives. However, it is not overly dependent on any one country as it is trying this in several places. It is now planning to build a proper naval base in Djibouti where even Americans have one. They enjoyed some facilities in Sri Lanka when Mahinda Rajapakse was in power. Though China has not been able to make any major breakthrough in the Maldives, Beijing is confident that its economic ties will help undercut political resistance. Beijing has also been encouraging Chinese tourists to visit Maldives as one of the economic incentives to the country. If the economic condition of Maldives deteriorates further, it would be compelled to turn to China for economic assistance.

The Maldivian policymakers agree that the country has opened up in the era of globalisation. Still, the Maldives has always prioritised its relationships. During Nasheed's period, India figured above China. China however figured above India during the Waheed's time. The situation has now somewhat started changing under the present regime of Abdualla Yameen. It is acknowledged in the Maldives that China has been very helpful in infrastructure building, particularly post the 2004 tsunami. The Maldives also benefits from China's potential in its tourism sector. The Maldivian policymakers recognise Chinese interests, and point out that India and China are not mutually exclusive.

China has not only been economically growing, it has also been expanding its outreach. They were pursuing their economic interests in Africa, while the world was busy fighting war on terror, and today, have an increased presence there. It has sensed an opportunity in a unipolar world, and is trying to fill the vacuum provided by the dismemberment of former Soviet Union.

To protect its various interests, China wants to develop multifaceted relationship with the Maldives. As Gayoom followed an open door policy to China, it had some success.[36] But things somewhat changed under Nasheed's regime, which also encouraged his opponents to accuse his government of avoiding China. During this period the most dominant view among the policymakers was that the Maldives should follow the 'India first' policy. This policy was never expressed in open terms but tacitly applied. The Maldivians at that point felt that their security was tied with South Asia's and were mindful of Sri Lankan and Indian security as well.

The Maldivian policymakers argue that while developing the relationship with China, the Maldivian Government always tries to ensure room for political, economic and diplomatic manoeuvres. But this space would dramatically shrink if the economic woes of the Maldives worsen and its dependence on China increases.

China has been interested in the IOR as its major energy supply vessels as well as its exports pass through it. It has been in search of new outlets to the Indian Ocean, and Myanmar, Bangladesh, and Gwadar (Pakistan) have figured prominently in its radar. Nevertheless, at present, China needs to secure the SLOCs in order to safeguard its interests in the IOR. The incumbent President of China, Xi Jinping, wants the country to become a maritime power, and for this reason, too, it might have to project power in the Indian Ocean, which connects the world. The new White Paper of Chinese defence also talks of protecting the overseas interests of China. This will inevitably require a blue water navy as Chinese interests become worldwide.

To protect their overseas interests, Chinese are also looking for overseas bases or at least facilities that can serve the same purpose. During the regime of the Sri Lankan President, Rajpakse, they had this facility in Sri Lanka where twice Chinese submarines were docked. They have been also spotted in the Gwadar Port of Pakistan. The Chinese are also planning to build their base in Djibouti. Though Chinese always had their eyes set on the Maldives, for a while the urgency to strengthen their hold on that country was reduced as they were making quick inroads in Sri Lanka. But now with the exit of Rajapakse, the Maldives has once again gained in importance. This was highlighted when the Chinese President, Xi Jinping, visited the Maldives in 2014 which was the first-ever visit of a Chinese

President to the archipelago nation since the former British protectorate gained independence in 1965.

Though China is liked by all regimes in the Maldives, the present regime likes China much more as it does not talk about the state of democracy in the country, nor about increasing Islamic radicalism. China, too, is happy to engage Maldives economically and militarily as it provides a strong foothold in the Indian Ocean.

The Chinese economy presently is the second-largest economy in the world. However, the double digit growth of Chinese economy is a thing of past, and it is slowing considerably now. To maintain peace at home and to gain the status of world power abroad, the Chinese need to grow at a fast pace. This economic growth they are now hoping to get through the export of infra projects. The Chinese Silk Route project is meticulously designed and conceived with the objective to give China the next round of growth. As mentioned earlier, the maritime component of the route is actually much bigger in comparison to the land route. Under the project, the Chinese are going to build a number of roads, railroad, ports, and other infrastructural facilities. The Chinese companies have already proven their prowess in this area.

The Chinese Silk Route project would also open up opportunity in another area of export of infrastructural projects which is different from commodity exports. This new strategy would come handy for the Chinese economy which is already suffering from problems of overproduction, and the US no longer remains a destination to invest capital profitably.

It is true that Chinese infrastructural projects are not always in the best interests of the receiving country. However, the Chinese have used diplomacy to good effect to sell these projects. But by the time receiving countries realise the trap it becomes too late. In the past, Myanmar has been a victim. Recently, similar concern was voiced by the incumbent President of Sri Lanka, Maithripala Sirisena, and a section in Pakistan. Unfortunately, barring Myanmar, most of these countries bought the idea of balancing India by bringing in China even at their own peril.

It has been suggested that Chinese Silk Route project is an answer to the US pivot to Asia.[37] Interestingly, so far the US pivot to Asia has not taken shape, but the Chinese counter to it seems to be doing quite well.

Both Sri Lanka and the Maldives have become willing partners of China in its MSR project which is going to majorly benefit China in the IOR.

The Indian Ocean has also been a prime area of interest for the US with its power centred around the main base in Deigo Garcia. In recent times, the US has however not been able to give attention to this region that it deserves. It is also true that despite the rise of China, the US remains the only military superpower in the world which has the ability and the willingness to engage in crises all over the world and shape the outcomes.[38] This has however also distracted the US which has spent too much time, energy, and resources on trouble spots like Afghanistan and Pakistan. The US is presently a superpower in disarray.

The US along with the UK and other nations of the European Union claimed to back the multi-party democracy in Maldives. However, it tried to sign a SOFA with the Maldives when Waheed was in power. It is also trying to intensify its relationship with the MNDF.

There is also an opinion in the Maldives that the country should have equally good relations with all three – India, the US, and China – in order to balance these major powers. To balance the US and other Western powers, the Maldivians are getting close to Saudi Arabia and China.

The closeness of Nasheed's regime to the UK and other Western powers had created a lot of misgivings among the Maldivians. Though Nasheed and the MDP had brought multi-party democracy to the Maldives, his association with the Conservative Party of Britain and his establishing of relationship with Israel was misconstrued as a threat to Islam. The US was in any case perceived as anti-Islam because of its involvement in the war against terror and its engagement in trouble spots like Afghanistan and Pakistan.

In this situation, they found China to be perfectly suiting their requirement. Moreover, China is also considered as a useful partner in trade, tourism, and infrastructure. This does not mean that Maldivians completely trust China and see it as a benign power. The Maldivian apprehension of China in fact had made Yameen to visit Japan, to counter the Chinese influence. There is also now considerable improvement in India's relationship with the Maldives.

The present foreign policy of the Maldives, as in the past, looks to benefit from everyone, but without ceding ground to anyone. However, what is different on this occasion is that now there are too many players in the great game to be managed. Presently, the Maldives seem to be managing the balancing act rather adroitly. But given the track record of China, it will not be easy for them to keep the Chinese out of the way for long. The Maldives along with some other countries of the Indian Ocean region is likely to see intense jostling for political and military influence.

NOTES

1. Iskander Rehman, "China's String of Pearls and India's Enduring Tactical Advantage," Institute for Defence Studies and Analyses, June 8, 2010, http://www.idsa.in/node/5468/413.
2. Anand Kumar, "China's Global Military Aspirations," *Indian Military Review*, 2, April 2011, p. 34.
3. Shen Dingli, "Don't Shun the Idea of Setting Up Overseas Military Bases," at http://www.china.org.cn/opinion/2010-01/28/content_19324522.htm.
4. Ibid.
5. "China Needs Overseas Bases for global role," *Global Times*, May 25, 2011, at http://opinion.globaltimes.cn/chinese-press/2011-05/658995.html.
6. The Ministry of Defence Annual Report, 1999-2000, said that "the location of the Republic of Maldives astride the major sealanes in the Indian Ocean is of strategic relevance to India". See the section on National Security Environment, at http://mod.nic.in/reports/report9901.htm.
7. "China: Base strategy - China Acquires a Base in Maldives against India with Some Help from Pakistan," *Dhivehi Observer,* at http://www.dhivehiobserver.com/speicalreports/China-base-in-Maldives0705051.htm.
8. This was confirmed to the author by a top official in the Maldivian Foreign Ministry; also see: "No Chinese Military Bases in Indian Ocean, Says Menon," *The Indian Express*, September 11, 2009, at http://www.indianexpress.com/news/no-chinese-military-bases-in-indian-ocean-s/516067/.
9. A top foreign policy advisor to the Maldivian Government in an interview to the author.
10. "Functional Translation of the Constitution of the Republic of Maldives 2008," p. 102, at http://www.maldivesinfo.gov.mv/home/upload/downloads/Compilation.pdf.
11. Rajat Pandit, "China's Stepped Up Moves in Maldives Worry India," *The Times of India*, October 11, 2011, at http://articles.timesofindia.indiatimes.com/2011-10-10/india/30262896_1_indian-military-surveillance-systems-ins-tillanchang-maldives.
12. A top foreign policymaker in an interview to the author.
13. Ahmed Moosa, Editor, *Haveeru Daily,* in an interview to the author.
14. Ibid.
15. N C Bipindra, "India, China in Hot Race to Build Maldives' Naval Dock," *The New Indian Express*, May 10, 2014, at http://www.newindianexpress.com/nation/India-China-in-Hot-Race-to-Build-Maldives-Naval-Dock/2014/05/10/article2216651.ece.

16. Azuhaar Abdul Azeez, "No 'Official' Proposal from India to Develop Dockyard, Says Minister," *Haveeru Online*, May 14, 2014, at http://www.haveeru.com.mv/news/54824.
17. Charu Sudan Kasturi, "Malé Assures Modi on China Footprint," *The Telegraph*, August 9, 2015, at http://www.telegraphindia.com/1150809/jsp/nation/story_36241.jsp#.VdQ5Y7Kqqko (Accessed August 19, 2015).
18. Mohamed Visham, "Indian Ocean Will Remain Demilitarized, Maldives Assures India," *Haveeru Online*, August 8, 2015, at http://www.haveeru.com.mv/news/61445 (Accessed August 19, 2015); also see: Indrani Bagchi, "Will Keep Indian Ocean Demilitarized: Maldives," *The Times of India*, August 10, 2015, at http://timesofindia.indiatimes.com/world/south-asia/Will-keep-Indian-Ocean-demilitarized-Maldives/articleshow/48417384.cms (Accessed August 19, 2015).
19. "China Says It Is Not Planning Military Bases in the Maldives," *The Hindu*, July 29, 2015, at http://www.thehindu.com/news/international/china-says-it-is-not-planning-military-bases-in-the-maldives/article7474682.ece?css=print (Accessed August 19, 2015).
20. "India Need Not Worry about China's Military Expansion in Maldives: State-run Media Report," *The Economic Times*, July 25, 2015, at http://economictimes.indiatimes.com/news/defence/india-need-not-worry-about-chinas-military-expansion-in-maldives-state-run-media-report/articleshow/48214133.cms?prtpage=1 (Accessed August 19, 2015).
21. Elisabeth Rosenthal, David E. Sanger, "U.S. Plane in China after It Collides with Chinese Jet," *The New York Times*, April 2, 2001 at http://www.nytimes.com/2001/04/02/world/us-plane-in-china-after-it-collides-with-chinese-jet.html?pagewanted=all
22. From the interview conducted by the author during the field visit.
23. N Sathiya Moorthy, "Maldives: Decision on 'US Military Base' May Have to Wait," *South Asia Weekly Report*, Observer Research Foundation, VI (22), June 03, 2013, at http://www.observerindia.com/cms/sites/orfonline/modules/weeklyassessment/WeeklyAssessmentDetail.html?cmaid=52834&mmacmaid=52835&volumeno=VI&issueno=22 (Accessed August 17, 2015).
24. "UN Chief Welcomes Report into Maldives' Transfer of Power, Urges Parties to Accept Findings," UN News Centre, August 30, 2012, at http://www.un.org/apps/news/story.asp?NewsID=42776#.VbXLELOqqko.
25. "Assistant Secretary for South and Central Asian Affairs Robert O. Blake Jr. Travels to Nepal, Maldives, and Sri Lanka," Media Note, Office of the Spokesperson, U.S. State Department, Washington, DC , September 7, 2012 at http://www.state.gov/r/pa/prs/ps/2012/09/197492.htm
26. "US hopes to sign SOFA with Maldives soon," *Haveeru*, May 07, 2013 at http://www.haveeru.com.mv/robert_blake/48862
27. "No proposal for US military base in Maldives, insists Minister," Abdullah Jameel, Haveeru Online, April 25, 2013 at http://www.haveeru.com.mv/news/48670
28. Mohammed Badrul Alam, "Strategic Perspective of India-Maldives Relations," Centre for Land Warfare Studies (CLAWS), New Delhi, October 28, 2015 at http://www.claws.in/1458/strategic-perspective-of-india-maldives-relations-dr-mohammed-badrul-alam.html
29. "India-Maldives joint military exercise concludes," The Hindu, September 14, 2015,

at http://www.thehindu.com/news/cities/Thiruvananthapuram/indiamaldives-joint-military-exercise-concludes/article7650540.ece

30. "India to Provide Helicopter and Hospital," *Miadhu Daily*, August 23, 2009, at http://www.miadhu.com.mv/2009/08/local-news/india-to-provide-helicopter-and-hospital/
31. "India to Help Defend Maldives," *Al Jazeera*, August 22, 2009, at http://english.aljazeera.net/news/asia/2009/08/2009821142254284884.html; also see: "Antony to Give Maldives Shield Against Terror?," August 20, 2009, at http://timesofindia.indiatimes.com/india/Antony-to-give-Maldives-shield-against-terror/articleshow/4912096.cms.
32. "DRP Advises Caution on Indian Media Claims," *Minivan News*, August 17, 2009, at http://www.minivannews.com/news_detail.php?id=7090.
33. With an eye on China, India sends aircraft carrier to Malé, TNN | Feb 14, 2016, at http://timesofindia.indiatimes.com/india/With-an-eye-on-China-India-sends-aircraft-carrier-to-Malé/articleshowprint/50979688.cms
34. Jayanta Gupta, "IOR littoral security tops fleet review agenda: Navy," The Times of India, 6 February, 2016, at http://timesofindia.indiatimes.com/city/kolkata/IOR-littoral-security-tops-fleet-review-agenda-Navy/articleshow/50872495.cms
35. A top policymaker of Maldives in an interview to author.
36. A top official of Maldivian Foreign Ministry in an interview to author.
37. Brahma Chellaney, "China Reinvents 'String of Pearls' as Maritime Silk Road," *Nikkei Asian Review*, April 29, 2015, at http://asia.nikkei.com/Viewpoints/Perspectives/China-reinvents-string-of-pearls-as-Maritime-Silk-Road.
38. John Ryan, "China and Indo-U.S. Relations: An Emerging Triangle? An Interview with Shivshankar Menon," The National Bureau of Asian Research, June 26, 2015, at http://www.nbr.org/research/activity.aspx?id=582 (Accessed August 17, 2015).

9

The Future of Democracy in Maldives and Its Impact on the Security Environment in the Indian Ocean Region

The Maldives' shift to a democratic government after the 2008 presidential elections was the culmination of the constitutional development process that had started in 1932. The world welcomed this Maldivian embrace to democracy and was watching closely how the Maldives managed Islam, thrust to modernity, and democracy. The country has been partly successful in this formidable task. Interestingly, the democratic transition of the Maldives also saw resurgence of the Islamist forces who used the democratic space available in the country to promote their cause. In fact, Islamists were a major factor behind the premature exit from power of the first democratically elected government of President Nasheed. President Abdulla Yameen however now seems to be following the policy of Gayoom days where the government tried to bolster its Islamic Identity and at the same time took action against ultra-radical forces who posed threat to the government.

The new constitution of 2008 which brought democracy in the Maldives faced some teething problems when the Nasheed government took charge. The most important problem was the division of power between the president and the parliament. Ideally, one may argue that it's a happy situation for democracy as each can act as a check to the other, and balance the situation. In practice, however, it proved to be a great hindrance, ultimately forcing Nasheed's cabinet to resign en masse. This also underlined the necessity for any incumbent president to control parliament if he wanted to function smoothly, given the adversarial politics that prevails in South Asia.

The multi-party democracy has also brought bitter struggle for power in the Maldives. In February 2012, Waheed conspired with the deep state in the Maldives and with the political rivals of Nasheed to overthrow him. It can be argued that the present government of Abdulla Yameen may not be reflecting the true will of the Maldivian people. Not only the democratic institutions of the Maldives were manipulated to further the political and electoral fortunes of Yameen, money was also blatantly used to buy out voters.

Undoubtedly, the Maldives needs to strengthen its democratic institutions. Though the multi-party democracy was implemented with the 2008 Constitution, the tools to implement and preserve it continued to reflect characteristics of the Gayoom era. The people recruited by him still dominate major institutions like the army, police, and judiciary. As a result, they are open to exploitation by undemocratic forces. This is exactly what happened after the first round of the 2013 presidential elections when Gasim Ibrahim of the Jumhooree Party unduly influenced the judiciary to annul the results.

It is true that the second multi-party elections in the Maldives may not have been completely free and fair, but they could prove to be an important step in the strengthening of democracy, provided future elections are held in a free, fair and inclusive manner. But, it seems presently Yameen is working on a strategy to weed out his political rivals, one by one.

The present government under President Yameen controls the parliament. Yameen through his machinations managed to bring the Jumhooree Party back in the coalition. He has misused administration to his advantage. He has engineered defection in the opposition ranks and many opposition MPs have now joined his PPM. Moreover, by misusing institutions he managed to jail Nasheed for 13 years and harmed the business interests of Gasim Ibrahim, who was once his ally and is now again willing to cooperate with him, possibly under duress. Clearly, the democracy in the Maldives is not in a healthy state, but still one can take solace from the fact that at least the archipelago nation has not reverted to the autocratic path by renouncing the present constitution.

Though India would like democracy to prevail in its neighbourhood, as democracy brings moderating influences over countries and societies, its approach should be such that does not bring chill in bilateral relationships. Chinese smartly say that they respect the system of governance chosen by other countries. This approach allows them easy entry in any country and helps them to promote their interests. India should also play a role in promoting democracy only when it is demand driven. Gayoom actually tilted towards China under the pressure of democratic movement in his country. He felt that a democratic India may not be the best bet for his political survival.

Now India needs to tread further cautiously in promoting democracy in the Maldives as the democratic transition in the country has coincided with greater rivalry for the control of the IOR. Now China has emerged as a major power, and is unwilling to depend on the US for protection of its 'overseas interests' which no longer remain limited to protection of the SLOCs. Moreover, there is a gradual expansion of China's national interests, and it wants its security forces to protect those national interests. The latest Chinese military strategy delineates an expansive China emerging as a maritime power. With this objective it is expanding its naval forces and developing a blue water navy, which would require access points in various parts of the world especially in the Indian Ocean where crucial Chinese interests are located. The Chinese are not only building a naval base at Djibouti, but are also eyeing the Maldives which is located at the centre of the Indian Ocean, and from where most of the important SLOCs pass through.

The Chinese maritime interests are likely to expand majorly once it is able to implement its MSR project. Besides India, a number of Southeast Asian countries are apprehensive about the MSR project, but this project has also attracted several island nations of the IOR, who see it as a great opportunity to get Chinese expertise in infrastructure building and also hope to get financed for the same. No wonder, both Sri Lanka and the Maldives have shown keen interest in the MSR project, which is also seen as a means to consolidate Beijing's influence in the IOR.

The attraction of China for the Maldives is however not limited only to the MSR project. It is already involved in a number of other infrastructural development activity in the Maldives. It managed to displace India's GMR group in 2013 from the $ 500 million Malé international airport project. This shows the influence of the Chinese over the present political dispensation in the Maldives.

The regime of Abdulla Yameen thinks that a greater engagement with China is in the strategic interests of the Maldives. The Chinese not only provide the largest number of tourists for a country whose economy critically depends on tourism, their presence is also seen as a way to balance the influence of India. The Maldives also seems to be drifting away from the US as it is perceived as anti-Islam.

The democratic transition of the Maldives has also coincided with the increasing economic difficulties of the country, primarily because of the slowdown in the world economy and corruption and mindless expansion of bureaucracy in the country over the years. Interestingly, the present government of Abdulla Yameen says that the economic crisis is because of the multi-party democracy which has created a number of new institutions, increasing the expenditure of the government and worsening the financial crisis.

While the reasons behind the economic crisis can be debated, the crisis has made the Maldives explore options that were previously unthinkable. The Maldives has now passed a constitutional amendment that allows the foreigners to get land on free-hold basis. It is widely perceived that the Maldives has taken this step to accommodate the Chinese who have developed an expertise in reclaiming land from the sea. These investments are however very expensive, worth minimum $ 1 billion, making it difficult for most projects to be economically viable. But the Chinese might still go for it considering larger strategic benefits.

Nevertheless, the way in which Chinese engagement with the Maldives is increasing soon it will become impossible for the country to benefit economically from China and still keep Chinese military interests out. The Chinese, of course, want to increase their hold over the Maldives, especially after losing their political influence in Sri Lanka and Myanmar

The Maldives, on its part, still claims that it sees its security interests through the lens of India and Sri Lanka, but other powers too want to be its security partners, namely China and the US. As mentioned earlier, the US attempted to sign a SOFA when Waheed was in power. While India assumed that its interests were better served with multi-party democracy and Nasheed in power, the Americans used the resultant strain in the bilateral relationship to promote their cause. Interestingly, while the Americans were negotiating SOFA with the Maldives, their Western partners stopped making noise over the democratic deficit in the country. Clearly, the Americans were willing to ignore the state of democracy in the Maldives for strategic advantage. This has discredited their democracy project in the Maldives which Nasheed is once again trying to rejuvenate after going to London taking prison leave.

Certainly, American presence in the Maldives would have dramatically changed the strategic landscape of the IOR. However, from the Indian perspective, to counter increasing Chinese naval presence in the Indian Ocean, welcoming increased US military presence in the region may not be a very judicious idea. It is not necessary that increased American military presence in the Indian Ocean region would be benign and to India's advantage. It may only create further complications for the Indian foreign policy towards the Maldives and worsen rivalry among external powers in the IOR.

India is trying to develop cooperative structures in the IOR through IORA, IONS, BIMSTEC, and more recently through the trilateral maritime agreement with Sri Lanka and the Maldives. However, the desire of China to become a maritime power has also brought in competition in this region. The Chinese are already trying to project power by sending submarines in the Indian Ocean. These submarines have docked at Colombo and Gwadar, and a submarine is also suspected to have travelled in the Maldivian waters.

In an environment of intensifying competition in the IOR, the effort of India should be to take greater responsibility commensurate with its status as a major regional power with potential to become a global power. India should build its naval power in such a way that gives the impression that it is a net provider of security in the IOR. For this, India needs an effective national maritime security strategy that creates a synergy between its foreign policy, the strength of Indian Navy, and the domestic defence and maritime industry which in turn can create lasting friendly relations with all littorals in the region.

APPENDICES

APPENDIX 1

Statement by His Excellency Mohamed Nasheed, President of the Republic of Maldives to the General Debate of the General Assembly

24 September 2009, New York

Mr. President,

Mr. Secretary-General, Excellencies, and Distinguished Delegates:

May I begin by extending to you, Mr President, my delegation's warmest congratulations on your election to preside over the Sixty-fourth Session of the General Assembly. I assure you of the full support and cooperation of my delegation.

May I also take this opportunity, to offer our most profound appreciation to your predecessor, His Excellency Mr Miguel Broekmann, for the exemplary manner in which he guided the work of the Sixty-third Session.

Allow me also to offer my delegation's heartfelt gratitude to Secretary-General Ban Ki-Moon, for his inspiring leadership and dedication in promoting the noble principles and ideals of this Organisation.

Mr. President,

This is the first statement to the General Assembly of a democratically-elected President of the Maldives. I am extremely pleased to be here. I have spent many of the past General Assembly sessions locked in a hot humid, damp cell with my hands shackled and my feet bound; imprisoned for my conviction that the 300,000 people of the Maldives should be free from fear, free from want and free to live their lives in liberty and in dignity.

Mr President:

I would like to thank the international community for their invaluable support in helping secure our democratic transition. Refooners in the Maldives and our friends in the United Nations should feel justffiably proud that our island home was able to mark last year's first International Day of Democracy in the best possible way—by throwing-o£f a thirty year-old autocracy and securing a smooth, peaceful and democratic transfer of power.

Just as the international community, played a key role in securing the Maldives' democratic transition, so, I hope, it will play a role in the even more difficult task of making sure our democracy becomes a permanent feature rather than a passing illusion. All of us who care about the Maldives and believe in democracy bear an enormous responsibility to ensure that the beliefs we fought for are set in stone rather than written in sand.

Mr President,

There are three areas in which the Maldives seeks the help of the international community. The first is continued collaboration in democracy-building. We must work together to strengthen the various pillars of a democratic society, namely human rights protection, good governance, independent oversight bodies, the free press, and civil society. The Maldives has made enormous progress across these pillars, but much remains to be done. My sense is that the necessary foundations are now in place.

Separation of powers has been established by constitutional reform A range of independent agencies and commissions have now been set-up. We have a thriving independent media. Nevertheless, several crucial challenges still remain and we look forward to the support of the international community as we move to meet these challenges.

In particular, I would like to stress the importance of ensuring equality of women and men, not just in name but *in* practice as well.

Mr President,

The second way in which the international community can help consolidate democracy and rule of law in the Maldives is by promoting a conducive economic environment. As a small and open market economy heavily dependent on tourism and fishery exports, the Maldives has suffered badly from the current global recession.

Moreover, since assuming office, it has become clear to us that in the run-up to last year's election, the former Government engaged in highly irresponsible economic policies *in* the hope of buying their way to victory. Add to this picture our continued efforts to recovery from the 2004 Tsunami, our impending graduation from the Least Developed Country category, and the high oil and food prices of recent years, and the scale of the economic challenge facing the new Government becomes apparent.

The new Government is determined to confront this challenge with honesty and with vigour. In consultation with the IMF and the World Bank, we have embarked on a programme of major economic reform designed to reduce the bloated public sector, privatise public utilities and promote private enterprise and trade. Yet the scale of the problems we face mean we cannot succeed on our own.

We therefore look to you, our friends in the international community, to help us get back onto our feet We are very grateful for the support extended to us by the IMF and the Indian Government to name but two. However, more is needed if democracy and human rights are to coexist with economic stability and prosperity.

Mr President,

The third way *in* which the international community can and must help the Maldives consolidate democracy and establish a secure, prosperous and equitable society, is by taking urgent and effective action to tackle global climate change.

The threats posed to the Maldives from climate change are well-known. Every beach lost to rising seas, every house lost to storm surges, every reef lost to the increasingly warm waters, every job lost as fish stocks dwindle, and every life lost to more frequent extreme weather events will make it harder and harder to govern the country until a point is reached when we must consider abandoning our homeland.

I therefore call on you, the leaders of the world, to protect the future of front-line countries like the Maldives by reaching an ambitious and effective agreement at December's UNFCCC conference in Copenhagen which seeks to limit average global temperature increases to less than 1.5 degrees centigrade above pre-industrial levels. To do otherwise would be to sign the death warrant for the 300,000 Maldivians,

But, the Maldives is determined to do what we can to survive. We are going to be the first country to go carbon-neutral in 10 years time. In order to do that, we are determined to formulate a survival-kit, a carbon-neutral manual that would enable others to replicate in order that all of us together might just about save ourselves from climate catastrophe.

As part of our efforts to achieve a unified voice, I will be inviting some of the most vulnerable states affected by climate change to the Maldives. We hope that this November summit will reinforce our determination to leave no stone unturned to ensure our survival.

Mr President,

I would like to now touch on a number of other important issues which are of enormous concern to us. The Maldives abhors terrorism in all its forms and is determined to stand shoulder-to-shoulder with all countries in facing down this menace. Events over the past year in Afghanistan, Pakistan and India, our neighbours and partners in South Asia, show us that victory in this fight will not be easily achieved.

They also show us that to effectively tackle terrorism, we must reaffirm not dilute our commitment to human rights, democracy, rule of law and good governance.

Mr. President,

While we applaud recent efforts to reform and revitalise the United Nations, we believe that such reforms cannot be successful or complete without the much-anticipated and much-need reform of the Security Council

We firmly believe that the third round of intergovernmental negotiations on Security Council reform must produce tangible results. I call upon the Assembly to complete this task during the 64th session, and agree on the increase of both permanent and non-permanent membership of the Council, In terms of composition, we believe that the geopolitical realities of the contemporary world must be duly reflected in the membership of Council. As such, we support the inclusion of India and Japan as Permanent Members of the Security Council.

Mn President,

The new Government of the Maldives is determined to pursue friendly and mutually respectful relations with every country represented in this room.

However, any friendship must include a willingness to be frank with one another and to object to behaviour not befitting of a sovereign State. We believe dialogue and constructive engagement serve the cause of peace better than ostracism and isolation. The new government in the Maldives will look to renew relations with Israel and to use the relationship to reiterate our support for an independent and sovereign Palestinian homeland, in conformity with the relevant resolutions of the UN Security Council.

Mr President,

The Maldives is seeking election to the United Nations Human Rights Council during the cuixent session of the General Assembly. We are doing so because we firmly believe in the universality of human rights and its critical importance *to* achieving the noble goals of the UN Charter.

Standing at this podium, I must admit how, as a prisoner, I was inspired by the courage and vision of Aung Sang Suu Kyi of Burma. Today, I would like to echo the call of the Secretary-General for her immediate and unconditional release along with all other political prisoners. I also reiterate my strident support for the work assigned to Mr Ibrahim Gambari, the UN Special Envoy to Burma, and say a prayer to political prisoners everywhere.

Mr President,

In conclusion, I must say that the most critical test so far of the resoluteness of the international community to save itself will come during your watch as President of this assembly: the Copenhagen meeting in

December. We must prime ourselves to succeed at that conference. Between now and then, Mr. President, we must all use every opportunity, every debate, every encounter to achieve that goal. It is imperative that we succeed If we want to save the world, saving the Maldives I suggest is a very good starting point.

I, thank you. Mr President

Appendix 2

Proposed Agreement between The United States of America and The Republic of Maldives Regarding Status of Forces and Access to and use of Facilities in the Maldives

The United States of America (hereinafter, "the United States") and the Republic of Maldives, hereinafter referred to collectively as "the Parties" and singularly as a "Party";

Seeking to advance the fense cooperation as reflected in recent discussions between representatives of the Parties regarding issues related to mutually agreed activies by United States Armed Forces in the Republic of Maldives;

Recalling the Acquisition and Cross-Servicing Agreement (US-MV-01) between the Department of Defense of the United States of America and the Maldives National Defense Force, signed in Kurumba, Maldives on September 22, 1016;

Have agreed as follows:

ARTICLE I
Definitions

1. "United States personnel" means members of the United States Armed Forces and civilian employees of the United States Department of Defense.
2. "United States forces" means the entity comprising United States

personnel and all property, equipment, and material of the United States Armed Forces present in the Republic of Maldives.

3. "United States contractors" means non-Maldivian companies and firms, and their employees who are not national of the Republic of Maldives, under contract to the United States Department of Defense.
4. "Agreed Facilities and Areas" means the facilities and areas in the territory and territorial seas of the Republic of Maldives provided by the Republic of Maldives and listed in Annex A hereto, and such other facilities and areas in the territory and territorial seas of the Republic of Maldives as may be provided by the Republic of the Maldives in the future, to which United States forces and United States contractors shall have the right to access and use pursuant to this Agreement.

ARTICLE II

Scope

This Agreement incorporates the principal provisions and necessary authorizations for the temporary presence and activities of United States forces in the Republic of Maldives and, in the specific situations indicated herein, the presence and activities of United States contractors in the Republic of Maldives.

ARTICLE III

Personnel Matters

1. United States personnel shall be accorded the privilleges, exemptions and immunities equivalent to those accorded to the administrative and technical staff of a diplomatic mission under the Vienna Convention on Diplomatic Relations of April 18, 1961.
2. The Republic of Maldives recognizes the particular importance of disciplinary control by United States Armed Forces authorities over United States personnel and, therefore, authorities the United States to exercise criminal jurisdiction over United States personnel while in the Republic of Maldives.
3. United States personnel shall be authorized to wear uniforms while performing official duties and to carry arms while on duty if authorized to do so by their orders.

4. United States personnel and United States contractors shall have freedom to movement and access to and use of agreed transportations, storage, training, and agreed facilities and areas in connection with activities under the Agreement.

ARTICLE IV
Entry and Exit

United States personnel may enter and exit the Republic of Maldives with United States identification and with collective movement or individual travel orders.

ARTICLE V
Licenses

1. The Republic of Maldives shall accept as valid all professional licenses issued by the appropriate United States authorities to United States personnel and United States contractors for the provision of services to authroised personnel.
2. The Republic of Maldives shall accept as valid, without a free or driving test, driving licenses or permits issued by the appropriate United States authorities to United States personnel and United States contractors for the operation of vehicles.

ARTICLE VI
Importation, Exportation and Taxes

1. United States personnel shall not be liable to pay any tax or similar charge assessed within the Republic of Maldives.
2. United States contractors shall not be liable to pay any tax or similar charge assessed within the Republic of Maldives in connection with activities under this Agreement.
3. United States personnel may import into, export out of, and use in the Republic of Maldives any personal property, equipment, supplies, materiel, technology, training, or services in connection with activities under this Agreement. Such importation, exportation, and use shall be exempt from any inspection, license, other restrictions, customs duties, taxes, or any other charges assessed within the Republic of Maldives.

4. United States contractors may import into, export, out of, and use in the Republic of Maldives any personal property, equipment, supplies, materiel, technology, training or services in fulfillment of contracts with United States forces in connection with activities under this Agreement. Such importation exportation, and use shall be exempt from any license, other restrictions customs duties, taxes or any other charges assessed within the Republic of Maldives.

ARTICLE VII

Security

The United States and the Republic of Maldives shall corporate to take such measures as may be necessary to ensure the security and protection of United States forces and official information in the Republic of Maldives.

ARTICLE VIII

Movement of Aircraft, Vehicles, and Vessels

1. Vessels and vehicles operated by or, at the time exclusively for United States forces may enter, exit and move freely within the territory and territorial seas of the Republic of Maldives, and such vehicles (whether self-propelled or towed) shall not be subject to the payment of overland transit tolls.
2. Vessels and aircraft owned or operated by or, at the time, exclusively for the United States shall not be subject to the payment of landing, parking, or port fees, pilotage charges, lighterage, and harbor dues at facilities owned and operated by the Government of the Republic of Maldives.
3. Aircraft owned and operated by or, at the time, exclusively for the United States shall not be subject to payment of navigation, overflight, terminal, or similar charges when in the territory of the Republic of Maldives.
4. United States forces shall pay reasonable charges for services requested and received at rates no less favorable than those paid by the Armed Forces of the Republic of Maldives.
5. Aircraft and vessels of the United States shall be free from boarding and inspection.

ARTICLE IX
Contracting

1. The United States may contract for any materiel, supplies, equipment, and services (including construction) to be furnished or undertaken in the Republic of Maldives without restriction as to choice of contractor, supplier, or person who provides such materiel, supplies, equipment, or services. Such contracts shall be solicited, awarded and administered in accordance with the laws and regulations of the United States.
2. Acquisition of articles and services in the Republic of Maldives by or on behalf of the United States in connection with activities under this Agreement shall not be subject to any taxes or similar charges in the Republic of Maldives.

ARTICLE X
Use of Agreed Facilities and Areas

1. The Republic of Maldives hereby provides and grants the United States access to and use of aerial ports, sea ports, and Agreed Facilities and Areas. United States forces may use such aerial ports, sea ports, and Agreed Facilities and Areas for: transit, support, and related activities; Bunkering of ships, refueling of aircraft; maintenance of vessels, aircraft, vehicles, and equipment, accommodation of personnel; communications; ship visits; training; exercises; humanitarian activities; and for such other purposes as the Parties may agree.
2. The Republic of Maldives authorises United States forces to exercise all rights and authorities within Agreed Facilities and Areas that are necessary for their use, operation, defense, or control, including the right to undertake new construction works and make alterations and improvements. United States personnel and United States contractors may carry out such construction, alterations, and improvements, As practicable and in consultation with the Republic of Maldives, the United States intends to use existing facilities in the Republic of Maldives without such construction, alterations, and improvements.
3. The Republic of Maldives hereby authorizes United States forces to control entry to Agreed Facilities and Areas that have been provided

for exclusive use by United States forces, and to coordinate entry with Republic of Maldives authorities at joint-use agreed facilities and areas, for purposes of safety and security. United States forces are hereby authorized to control activities in the vicinity of each such Agreed Facility and Areas as United States personnel determine are necessary to ensure the safety of United States forces and United States contractors and to secure such facilities and areas.

4. The Republic of Maldives shall furnish, without charge to the United States, all Agreed Facilities and Areas, including facilities and areas jointly used by the United States and the Republic of Maldives.
5. Unless otherwise agreed by the Parties, the United States shall be responsible for the construction, development, operations, and maintenance costs for Agreed Facilities and Areas provided for the exclusive use of United States forces. Construction, development, operations and maintenance costs for Agreed Facilities and Areas provided for joint use, or otherwise used jointly, shall be shared on the basis of proportionate use, unless otherwise agreed.

ARTICLE XI
Telecommunications

The Republic of Maldives recognizes that it may be necessary for United States forces to use the radio spectrum. United States forces shall be allowed to operate its own telecommunication systems (as telecommunication is defined in the 1992 Constitution and Convention of the International Telecommunication Union). This shall include the right to utilize such means and services as required to ensure fall ability to operate telecommunication systems, and the right to use all necessary radio spectrum for this purpose. Use of the radio spectrum shall be free of cost to the United States.

ARTICLE XII
Claims

Each Party waives any and all claims (other than contractual claims) against the other for damage to, loss of, or destruction of its property or injury or death to personnel of either Party's armed forces or their civilian personnel arising out of the performance of their official duties in connection with activities under this Agreement. Claims by third parties for damages or loss caused by United States personnel shall be resolved by the United States in accordance with United States laws and regulations.

ARTICLE XIII
Property Ownership

1. The Republic of Maldives shall retain ownership of, and title to, Agreed Facilities and Areas owned by the Republic of Maldives.
2. The United States shall return to the Republic of Maldives any Agreed Facility or Areas, or portion thereof, including non-relocatable structure and assemblies constructed, modified, or improved by the United States, once no longer required by United States forces. The Parties shall consult regarding the terms of return of any Agreed Facility and Area, including possible compensation for improvements or construction.
3. Notwithstanding the terms of this Article, United States personnel and United States constructors shall return title to all equipment, materials, supplies, relocatable structures, and other properties they have imported into or acquired within the Republic of Maldives in connection with this Agreement.

ARTICLE XIV
Implementation

1. The Parties may enter into implementing arrangements to carry out the provisions of this Agreement. In the event of conflict between an implementing arrangement and this Agreement, the terms of this Agreement shall govern.
2. The obligations of the United States under this Agreement are subject to the availability of appropriated funds authorized for such proposes.

ARTICLE XV
Settlement of Disputes

All disputes shall be resolved exclusively through consultation between the Parties. Disputes and other matters subject to consultation under this Agreement shall not be referred to any national or international court, tribunal, or similar body, or to any third party for settlement, unless otherwise mutually agreed.

ARTICLE XVI

Entry into Force, Amendment, and Termination

1. This Agreement shall enter into force on the date of the last note exchanged between the Parties, through diplomatic channels, indicating that their respective internal requirements for entry into force of the Agreement have been satisfied.
2. Upon entry into force, this Agreement shall supersede the Agreement between the Parties regarding Military and Department of Defense Civilian Personnel, effected by the Exchange of Notes on December 31, 2004,
3. The Parties may amend this Agreement at any time with mutual consent, and such amendments shall enter into force in accordance with Paragraph 1 of this Article.
4. This Agreement shall have an initial term of ten years, and thereafter, it shall continue in force automatically unless terminated by either Party upon one year's written notice to the other Party through diplomatic channels.

IN WITNESS WHEREOF, the undersigned, being duly authorized by their respective Governments, have signed this Agreement.

DONE at ______________, ____________, in duplicate in English, this __________ day of ________________, 20___.

FOR THE	FOR THE
UNITED STATES OF AMERICA	REPUBLIC OF MALDIVES

Appendix 3

Outcome Document of the Second NSA-Level Meeting on Trilateral Cooperation on Maritime Security between India, the Maldives and Sri Lanka

July 09, 2013

1. The Second NSA-level Meeting on Trilateral Cooperation on Maritime Security between India, the Maldives and Sri Lanka (hereinafter referred to as the 'Trilateral Meeting') took place in Colombo on 8, July 2013. The Indian side was led by H E Shivshankar Menon, National Security Advisor to the Prime Minister, Republic of India, the Maldivian side by Hon Mohamed Nazim, Minister of Defence and National Security of the Republic of Maldives and the Sri Lanka side by Mr Gotabaya Rajapaksa, Secretary, Ministry of Defence and Urban Development of the Democratic Socialist Republic of Sri Lanka (hereinafter referred to as the 'three sides').
2. Following the First NSA-level Trilateral Meeting in Male on 1 October 2011, four meetings were held at the senior official and technical level between the three sides. This preparatory work has been useful in framing the outcomes of the Second NSA-level Trilateral Meeting.
3. During the Second NSA-level Trilateral Meeting, the three sides discussed a wide range of topics including enhancing cooperation in Maritime Domain Awareness (MDA) through provision of Long Range Identification and Tracking (LRIT) services, MDA training

and Merchant Ship Information System (MSIS) software by India, sharing of Automatic Identification System (AIS) data; strengthening coordination of maritime Search and Rescue (SAR) including SAR training; promoting marine oil pollution response cooperation; expanding bilateral 'DOSTI' (friendship) exercises through holding of table top exercises; further enhancing sharing of the information on illegal maritime activities through existing points of contact; and forming a trilateral sub-group focused on policy and legal issues related to piracy. The roadmap for future cooperation in all these areas was confirmed and is outlined below:

I. obtain the facility of the Indian Long Range Identification and Tracking (LRIT) Data Centre by Sri Lanka and Maldives in order to monitor and track Maldives and Sri Lanka flagged merchant vessels owned by them. Sri Lanka and Maldives are to provide required details as per International Maritime Organisation (IMO) regulations through diplomatic channels;

II. utilisation of the Merchant Ship Information System (MSIS) for exchange of unclassified information on white shipping;

III. sharing Automatic Identification System (AIS) data in a trilateral format over the MSIS platform;

IV. undertaking Maritime Domain Awareness (MDA) training in India;

V. strengthening maritime linkages in the field of Search and Rescue (SAR) including through SAR operations, providing expertise and technical assistance by India in setting up Maritime Rescue Coordination Centres (MRCCs) in Sri Lanka and Maldives, coordination in relaying and receiving distress alerts and safety messages, and, conduct of SAR training in India;

VI. strengthening mechanisms for Exclusive Economic Zone (EEZ) surveillance and providing additional support and assets on a case by case basis;

VII. maintaining lines of communication on illegal maritime activities between identified Points of Contact and exchanging messages on a regular basis;

VIII. strengthening marine pollution response cooperation through conduct of IMO Level I and Level II courses in India, formulating Contingency Plans for pollution response, capacity building, and participating in India's National Pollution Response Exercise (NATPOLREX), as observers;

IX. strengthening the biennial trilateral exercise 'DOSTI' by conducting table top exercises and seminars on maritime issues in every alternate year;

X. passing Tsunami warnings simultaneously to agreed Points of Contact in addition to the designated National Tsunami Warning Centres;

XI. setting up a trilateral sub-group focused on legal and policy issues related to piracy.

4. The three sides agreed that in the current maritime security environment in the Indian Ocean Region (IOR), it was important to raise the level of maritime cooperation between India, the Maldives and Sri Lanka. In this context, it was also agreed to explore the possibility of expanding the scope of the trilateral initiative to include other Indian Ocean littoral countries.

5. The three sides agreed that the Third NSA-level Trilateral Meeting will be convened at a mutually convenient date in 2014 to review the progress made in implementing the areas of cooperation agreed upon as well as identifying new areas of cooperation. They also agreed that prior to the Third NSA-level Trilateral Meeting, the Working Group would meet to implement the consensus and decisions agreed to by the three sides at the Second NSA-level Trilateral Meeting.

Done at Colombo on 8, July 2013 in three originals.

Shivshankar Menon National Security Advisor to the Prime Minister for the Republic of India	Mohamed Nazim Minister of Defence & National Security for the Republic of Maldives	Gotabaya Rajapaksa RWP RSP psc Secretary of Defence & Urban Development for the Democratic Socialist Republic of Sri Lanka

Source: Ministry of External Affairs, Government of India, at http://www.mea.gov.in/bilateral-documents.htm?dtl/21922/Outcome+Document+of+the+Second+NSALevel+ Meeting +on+Trilateral+Cooperation+on+Maritime+Security+between+India+the+Maldives+and+Sri+Lanka

APPENDIX 4
MALDIVES

SUMMARY STATISTICS

Region	Southern Asia
Surface area (sq km)	300
Population (est., 000)	352
Pop. density (per sq km)	1179.8
Capital city	Male
Capital city pop. (000)	156
Currency	Rufiyaa (MVR)
UN membership date	21 September 1965

ECONOMIC INDICATORS

GDP: Gross domestic product (million current US$)	2013	2836
GDP: Gross domestic product (million current US$)	2010	2335
GDP: Gross domestic product (million current US$)	2005	1091
GDP: Growth rate at constant 2005 prices (annual %)	2013	3.7
GDP: Growth rate at constant 2005 prices (annual %)	2010	6.9
GDP: Growth rate at constant 2005 prices (annual %)	2005	-9.1
GDP per capita (current US$)	2013	8220.0
GDP per capita (current US$)	2010	7169.0
GDP per capita (current US$)	2005	3665.6
GNI: Gross national income per capita (current US$)	2013	6779.5

GNI: Gross national income per capita (current US$)	2010	6185.1	
GNI: Gross national income per capita (current US$)	2005	3434.9	
Gross fixed capital formation (% of GDP)	2013	15.9	
Gross fixed capital formation (% of GDP)	2010	26.2	
Gross fixed capital formation (% of GDP)	2005	34.5	
Exchange rates (national currency per US$)	2013	15.41	Market rate.
Exchange rates (national currency per US$)	2010	12.80	Market rate.
Exchange rates (national currency per US$)	2005	12.80	Market rate.
Balance of payments, current account (million US$)	2013	-176	
Balance of payments, current account (million US$)	2010	-196	
Balance of payments, current account (million US$)	2005	-273	
CPI: Consumer price index (2000=100)	2013	191	Male.
CPI: Consumer price index (2000=100)	2010	146	Male.
CPI: Consumer price index (2000=100)	2005	107	Male. Series linked to former series.
Agricultural production index (2004-2006=100)	2013	64	
Agricultural production index (2004-2006=100)	2010	72	
Agricultural production index (2004-2006=100)	2005	89	
Food production index (2004-2006=100)	2013	64	
Food production index (2004-2006=100)	2010	72	
Food production index (2004-2006=100)	2005	89	
Unemployment (% of labour force)	2013	11.6	
Unemployment (% of labour force)	2010	11.7	
Unemployment (% of labour force)	2005	13.4	
Employment in industrial sector (% of employed)	2013	...	
Employment in industrial sector (% of employed)	2010	...	
Employment in industrial sector (% of employed)	2005	24.3	2006. Population census. ISIC Rev.3. Excluding conscripts.
Employment in agricultural sector (% of employed)	2013	...	

Employment in agricultural sector (% of employed)	2010	...	
Employment in agricultural sector (% of employed)	2005	11.5	2006. Population census. ISIC Rev.3. Excluding conscripts.
Labour force participation, adult female pop. (%)	2013	56.2	
Labour force participation, adult female pop. (%)	2010	55.1	
Labour force participation, adult female pop. (%)	2005	50.2	
Labour force participation, adult male pop. (%)	2013	77.5	
Labour force participation, adult male pop. (%)	2010	76.4	
Labour force participation, adult male pop. (%)	2005	74.6	
Tourist arrivals at national borders (000)	2013	1125	Arrivals by air.
Tourist arrivals at national borders (000)	2010	792	Arrivals by air.
Tourist arrivals at national borders (000)	2005	395	Arrivals by air.
Energy production, primary (Petajoules)	2013	0	2012.
Energy production, primary (Petajoules)	2010	0	
Energy production, primary (Petajoules)	2005	0	
Mobile-cellular subscriptions (per 100 inhabitants)	2013	181.2	
Mobile-cellular subscriptions (per 100 inhabitants)	2010	151.8	
Mobile-cellular subscriptions (per 100 inhabitants)	2005	68.4	
Individuals using the Internet (%)	2013	44.1	ITU estimate.
Individuals using the Internet (%)	2010	26.5	Population aged 15 and over.
Individuals using the Internet (%)	2005	6.9	Country estimate. Excluding mobile Internet users.
Exports (million US$)	2013	166.5	

Imports (million US$)	2013	1733.3	
Balance (million US$)	2013	-1566.8	
Major trading partners (% of exports)	2013	Thailand (37.1), France (13.5), Iran (6.5)	
Major trading partners (% of imports)	2013	United Arab Emirates (28.4), Singapore (16.2), India (8.9)	
SOCIAL INDICATORS			
Population growth rate (average annual %)	2010-15	1.9	
Urban population growth rate (average annual %)	2010-15	4.5	
Rural population growth rate (average annual %)	2010-15	-0.1	
Urban population (%)	2014	44.5	
Population aged 0-14 years (%)	2014	28.4	
Population aged 60+ years (females and males, % of total)	2014	6.6/7.0	
Sex ratio (males per 100 females)	2014	101.3	
Life expectancy at birth (females and males, years)	2010-15	78.8/ 76.7	
Infant mortality rate (per 1 000 live births)	2010-15	10.4	
Fertility rate, total (live births per woman)	2010-15	2.3	
Contraceptive prevalence (ages 15-49, %)	2007-13	34.7	
International migrant stock (000 and % of total population)	mid-2013	84.2/ 24.4	Refers to foreign citizens.
Education: Government expenditure (% of GDP)	2007-13	6.2	
Education: Primary-secondary gross enrolment ratio (f/m per 100)	2007-13	102.4/ 100.7	UNESCO estimate. 2004
Education: Female third-level students (% of total)	2007-13	52.5	
Intentional homicide rate (per 100,000 population)	2008-12	3.9	
Seats held by women in national parliaments (%)	2015	5.9	
ENVIRONMENT			
Threatened species	2014	69	
Forested area (% of land area)	2012	3.0	

Proportion of terrestrial and marine areas protected (%)	2014	0.1
Population using improved drinking water sources (%)	2012	99.0
Population using improved sanitation facilities (%)	2012	99.0
CO_2 emission estimates (000 metric tons and metric tons per capita)	2011	1104/ 3.3
Energy supply per capita (Gigajoules)	2012	56.0

Source: World Statistics Pocketbook | United Nations Statistics Division at http://data.un.org/CountryProfile.aspx?crName=MALDIVES

INDEX